MORE PRAISE FOR
I WANNA BE WELL

"Miguel Chen's *I Wanna Be Well* is an honest and thoughtful approach to mindfulness. The book is full of insight and succinct ideas for anyone looking to expand their viewpoint and live well. A comfortable and fun read for intellectual and pinhead punks alike."

—TREVER KEITH, SINGER FOR FACE TO FACE

"*I Wanna Be Well* is a calming experience—empathy and love and punk and passion and weirdness."

—JOHNNY BONNEL, SINGER FOR SWINGIN' UTTERS

"*I Wanna Be Well* offers a spirituality grounded in tour buses and punk rock. From everyday scenarios to personal accounts, Miguel demonstrates a tangible practice founded in reality that is available anywhere, anytime. We live in uncertain times, with experiences from cruelty to beauty and all that lies in between—within it all, Miguel lets us know that we, too, can be well."

—SHARON SALZBERG, AUTHOR OF *REAL LOVE*

I WANNA
BE WELL

HOW A PUNK
FOUND PEACE
AND YOU CAN TOO

MIGUEL CHEN

with Rod Meade Sperry

Wisdom

Wisdom Publications
199 Elm Street
Somerville, MA 02144 USA
wisdompubs.org

Library of Congress Cataloging-in-Publication Data

Names: Chen, Miguel, author. | Meade Sperry, Rod, author.
Title: I wanna be well: how a punk found peace and you can too / Miguel Chen;
    with Rod Meade Sperry.
Description: Somerville, Ma: Wisdom Publications, [2018] |
Identifiers: LCCN 2017018175 (print) | LCCN 2017053184 (ebook) | ISBN 9781614294078
    (ebook) | ISBN 1614294070 (ebook) | ISBN 9781614293910 (pbk.: alk. paper)
Subjects: LCSH: Spiritual life—Buddhism.
Classification: LCC BQ5662 (ebook) | LCC BQ5662 .C44 2018 (print) |
    DDC 294.3/444—dc23
LC record available at https://lccn.loc.gov/2017018175

ISBN 978-1-61429-391-0   ebook ISBN 978-1-61429-407-8

22 21 20 19 18
5 4 3 2 1

Cover design by John Yates. Photo of Rod Meade Sperry by Liza Matthews. Set in
Trivia Serif 10 8.75/14.

Wisdom Publications' books are printed on acid-free paper and meet the
guidelines for permanence and durability of the Production Guidelines for
Book Longevity of the Council on Library Resources.

♻ This book was produced with environmental mindfulness. For more
information, please visit wisdompubs.org/wisdom-environment.

Printed in the United States of America.

Please visit fscus.org.

Contents

Preface   vii

1. Who Am I?   1
2. Who Are You?   7
3. Everything Sucks   15
4. On the Impossible Past   23
5. The Future Ain't What It Used to Be   31
6. Your Perfect Day   39
7. Wake Up   49
8. Breathe   57
9. I Wanna Be Well   63
10. Together Again for the First Time   69
11. A Juvenile Product of the Working Class   75
12. Give Freely   81
13. Change   87
14. Opportunity   95
15. Bullshit   101
16. Sorry Song   107
17. Finer Points of Forgiveness   115
18. I Like Food   121
19. Let's Talk about Feelings   127
20. Music   133
21. Yoga for Everybody   139
22. I Don't Wanna Grow Up   147
23. Bare-Bottom Thanking   155

24. Even on the Worst Nights   161

25. Rest in Peace   167

26. Your Perfect Day (Reprise)   171

Some Recommended Reading   173

Acknowledgments   175

About the Authors   177

Preface

LET'S BE HONEST, being a human can seem pretty awful sometimes.

My hope for this book was that it might help some people find relief from what I kind of like to call the "suckage" of life. In some ways things sure seem to suck a lot worse than they did at other times in recent memory. Hate and fear are definitely palpable in the air these days. Let me assure you, though, that I don't mean for this book to be political—and, really, it won't be. Suffice it to say this: There's a lot of suffering in the world—especially now.

Even so, our lives don't have to be *totally* miserable. Yeah, it sometimes seems there's an untenable amount of hate in the world. But even amid urgent and real global, social, and societal problems, there's stuff we can do to start to find a little peace in the here and now.

The key is love. Always has been, always will be. We need to open our hearts, standing by our brothers and sisters who are suffering. We need to try to understand those who are stuck in fear and hate and show them that there's a way out. We need to protect our earth, and each other. We need to take action.

There are many kinds of action we might take, but none of it will be possible if we don't work to cultivate kindness and compassion on all levels, beginning with ourselves and moving outward to include all beings.

That, ultimately, is what this book is about: doing that work, and being of benefit, whether the suffering we face is on the personal, private level or of a more societal, big-scale scope. All suffering is worth working to alleviate.

May we all return to our hearts and build a peaceful world for all of our brothers and sisters.

May love conquer hate.

1.

Who Am I?

IT'S A QUESTION we all need to ask ourselves. I'll get things started.

My name is Miguel Chen. I was born in Mexico and moved to the United States when I was three. I play bass in a punk-rock band called Teenage Bottlerocket. I own and teach at Blossom Yoga Studio in Laramie, Wyoming. I love dogs, horror movies, cooking/eating tacos, and watching baseball. I've often described myself as a spiritually inclined punk rocker, walking somewhere along what's called the Middle Path. Geez—this is starting to read like a dating site profile.

That's the problem—all these *words* describe who I am and what I am doing here, but at the end of it they're all just *words*. None of these things is really *who* I am.

So *who am I?*

I'm just a dude, just a person trying to navigate his way through this life like anyone else. I may be spiritually inclined, but I'm no spiritual master or enlightened being. (I'm not even sure such a thing exists.) I love, I get angry, I have my ups and downs like anyone else—like you.

I have fucked up a lot in the past, and I'm sure I will continue to do so. But I am also someone who wants to know peace and be happy. I am someone who believes we are all brothers and sisters on this earth—and so I want *you* to be happy too. I even think that you—yes, you—can have a perfect day, even when everything sucks. That might sound like some hippie shit to you. Maybe it is, but I don't care. My life has taught me that we are all more connected than we think. We're part of something bigger than ourselves.

Those connections are what life is all about.

For as long as I can remember all I ever wanted was to play music, travel, and hang with my friends. After years of being in shitty bands, writing terrible songs, and basically having no idea what the fuck I was doing, things started to line up. After a series of fortunate events—and a shit-ton of hard work—my dream became reality.

About ten years ago, I was lucky enough to be asked to join my favorite band: Teenage Bottlerocket. Ray, Brandon, Kody, and I all loved the same music and shared the same dreams, and so we worked and worked. We lived in our van, played wherever we could, and strived to perfect our craft.

And it worked! The band gained moderate success. We went on tours all over the world, put out records on a few different labels, and got to befriend and tour with many of our favorite bands. Sure, we never sold a million records or anything, but we were living the dream and doing what we'd always wanted to do.

But something seemed to be missing, and I began to suspect that seeking happiness outside of myself was a lost cause. I'd traveled the world, but now it was time to journey inward.

My mother had been a spiritual person when I was growing up, but—being a rebellious little jerk—I decided that if my mom liked something, then it probably wasn't for me. I couldn't appreciate her wisdom and her practice. It wouldn't be until many years after her passing that spirituality made its way back into my life.

So there I was, on top of my punk-rock dreams, yet suffering deeply. I couldn't understand it. So I began to search for an answer. Two events, featuring two people and two books, were pivotal.

The first of these events wasn't exactly welcome to begin with. My close friend Ben's mother decided she'd had enough of my bullshit. Jean was what most of us considered "the fun mom." Her son Ben and I grew up together. Their house was the place where we could stay up late, play music, and get into trouble—without getting into *too* much of it. All that changed one day when I was running around being a little jerk, as was my tradition back then.

Jean pulled me inside and chewed my ass out. I was addicted to drama, she told me, always creating problems for myself and those around me, and it was time for me to knock that shit off. She gave me a book called *The Four Agreements*, made me promise to read it, and sent me on my way.

My initial reaction was, *Man, fuck Jean—and her book.*

That feeling, thankfully, didn't last.

What I found in that book would begin to change me. After a long, slow process I realized Jean had been right: I *was* full of shit, I *was* addicted to drama, and I *did* need to wake up. Jean, if you're reading this, *thank you.*

The second event was much more welcome. TBR was out on tour with a wonderful band called the Epoxies. I made a strong connection with their lead singer, Roxy, a friendship I maintain to this day. Roxy could tell I was hurting. We would have lots of late-night talks about life, loss, happiness, and suffering. She gave me a copy of Noah Levine's memoir, *Dharma Punx*, and it immediately spoke to me. Suddenly, I'd found the meeting point between the spiritual world my mother had lovingly tried to show me and my punk-rock life.

I was hooked. I'd read every book I could get my hands on, watch every video, talk to everyone I could, and spend time every single day sitting my ass down on a meditation cushion and paying attention to my breathing.

As self-study and mindfulness became the foundation of my practice, my life began to transform. That's not to say that suddenly everything was perfect and I never suffered again. I still work at my life every day, with some days better than others, and I often find myself stuck in cycles of self-defeat and struggle. Now, though, I can recognize my struggles as part of the path. Even when things get so bad it seems they might never be okay again, I feel a subtle connection to a deeper part of myself, a part that knows everything is happening exactly as it was supposed to.

As my practice grew, something changed inside me: my heart began to open up. I realized that life wasn't just about me; it's about all of us. Loving ourselves is important, but it's only half the story. We've got to love others too. Suddenly, playing shows wasn't just about living out my punk dreams; it became a work of gratitude. I saw that music, even my music, can help people find moments of peace and raw connection in which everything is right with the universe. It was humbling to start to see that—and I still feel that way at every show, whether there are fifty people there or five thousand. I am lucky to do something I love, in a way that makes others happy.

After a while, my sense of gratitude and desire to help others began to spread into other areas of my life. I began to talk about my spiritual practice with anyone who would listen. I didn't think I had all the answers, but I still wanted to offer what I could in case it would help.

I've since become a certified yoga teacher and bought the yoga studio I'd long attended in Laramie, Wyoming. I've even started teaching yoga to crowds at punk festivals and shows, bringing together these two things I love. As all this began to get coverage, I took to social media—not just to promote myself but to try to be a voice of unity and positivity. From there, I got the opportunity to write some articles and, now, this book. I am so grateful.

IN BUDDHISM there is the concept of the *bodhisattva*, a being who dedicates her- or himself to freeing others from suffering. The bodhisattva knows that as long as one being suffers, we all suffer, because we are all connected. I've always loved that idea.

I am not saying that I'm some sort of selfless being. Nope—still just a dude. But I think the bodhisattva ideal is something we can all bring into our lives. The notion that we are all one—and must be kind to each other, because to be cruel to another is to be cruel to oneself—is an idea that can change the world. And it applies to punk rockers, Buddhist monks, cowboys, hippies, moms, dads, nurses, cops, soldiers . . . or whomever. It's an idea that can help literally anyone truly connect with the world around them.

In my time on this earth I have encountered many simple practices that have helped me connect and find happiness in the present moment. This book collects these practices so you can check them out for yourself. After all, if they can work for me, they can work for you!

I hope this book will be of benefit.

Okay, that's enough about me for a while.

Now: who are *you*?

2.

Who Are You?

IF YOU'RE READING THIS BOOK, it's a safe bet you're looking for something. Maybe you're unhappy, stuck, bored, lost—there's no limit to the ways we might feel dissatisfied in life. Perhaps you're looking for advice or direction on how to find your own happiness. (Or maybe you're my dad and you just bought this book to support me. If so: *Hi, Dad! Love you!*)

Whoever you are, let's begin with a simple question: just *who are you?*

Many spiritual practices lead us to ask this question, but it's not easy to answer. Well, I guess it *is* easy to answer . . . it's just not easy to answer *well.*

You might be quick to offer up basic descriptors like parent, adult, middle class, business professional, music lover, man, woman . . . but to do so would be to sell yourself short. Yes, you may be any of these things, and it's common for us to describe ourselves by what we do, but the truth is that we're all much greater than these words can ever express. Our jobs, likes, dislikes, or roles in society aren't the whole picture of *who we actually are.*

Some things, we all have in common. We are all human beings. We all have thoughts and bodies. We all feel happiness, sadness, anger, love. But *who* exactly is feeling all of these things? If your likes and dislikes, your job, your role, even your body and thoughts went away, *who* would be left?

You've probably had the inkling at one point or another that we are somehow more than our bodies. It's a fairly common idea. A less common but very interesting one is that we are also *not our thoughts.* In some spiritual traditions we are taught about the difference between the ego and the self. Ego in that case indicates where our thoughts come from. It's a tool that helps us navigate life on this earth. The self is something else—something more. And our thoughts? They're just something that happens; they are not who we are.

Thanks to my own spiritual practice, I've come to some semblance of an understanding of *who* we actually are. It goes something like this: We are all, everyone and everything, part of one thing. We're *interconnected.* (I am far from the first to say that, of course, but everything changed when I saw it for myself.) And *everything that has ever happened* is exactly what brought us here, where we are, as we are now. In this sense we are all connected more than we realize.

Our bodies may stop breathing and living, but this "something more" that we're all part of never dies. It simply changes forms. Take for example a piece of wood that's been lit on fire. After a while, it won't be that piece of wood anymore—it'll just be a little pile of ash and some fumes. But it's not *nothing.* All of the energy that composed it still exists, just in different forms. People might be seen the same way.

Another thing you should know about your deeper self—and everyone else's, for that matter—is that it is, at its foundational level, *good.* I know it might not always seem that way. It's often easy to get down on ourselves and forget this, but we are good at our core. I know this can be an incredibly hard concept to buy into. Many of us have spent our entire lives disconnected from this truth. Still, I believe that a part of you, no matter how buried, knows this. My hope is by the end of this book that part can come out of hiding, and you can catch a glimpse of your inner goodness.

This fundamentally good part of us—what's in our hearts when you take away all the stress and conditioning that's hardened them—can be said to be love. When we drop our judgments and quiet our mind, we can begin to reconnect with that part of ourselves. Spiritual practice in general and this book in particular are all about reconnecting to this core goodness—in ourselves, in others, in the world around us.

Yes, you are unique: after all, you're the only you there is. But you're also part of something bigger. Only you will experience what you experience, and it's up to you to use it all as a means of connection, rather than disconnection. It's up to you to use your unique gifts, attributes, and circumstances to connect with and benefit others.

But how? Is there a template for living well? No.

Allow me to elaborate: fuck no.

No two beings are ever the same, so what works for some, if you ask me, will never work for all. It's up to each of us to explore what works and what doesn't work in our lives.

But there *are* some things we all can and should do. You know: *don't murder each other; don't take what's not given to you freely; don't hurt others* . . . and so on. These ideas can be found in pretty much every religion—pretty much every society, really—and there's a great reason for that: our interconnectedness dictates that when we hurt others, we're also hurting ourselves. Beyond that, though, your uniqueness means that your truth won't look like anyone else's and that the possibilities are endless. This is great news!

Of course, you may be skeptical of all this. That's natural. After all, many people misunderstand what spiritual practice is about. Many people think it's about living on a mountain, giving up all worldly possessions, and meditating until you "leave your body." It can be those things, but there is no one set of rules.

This means you can hold on to the things you enjoy. You don't have to give anything up to benefit from spiritual practice. You can still eat meat, drink booze, smoke cigarettes, whatever. It's your life, your health, your call. Anyway, none of those things is who you are; they're just things you might happen to do.

For now, though, the first thing to do is learn how to sit down, breathe, and give yourself a moment to filter through life's bullshit and reconnect. This brings us to our first practice: a simple yet powerful meditation practice. It will be the foundation for many of the other practices in the book, but it's so valuable in and of itself that if it were all you got out of this book, you'd still be in good shape. Here's how I teach it.

■ ■ ■

Practice: Basic Meditation

Find somewhere quiet, free from distraction, and sit comfortably. Traditionally this is done on a cushion, or bench, with your legs in a variety of different postures. Many traditions think they've got the one way to sit nailed and others simply aren't doing it right. I call bullshit. The only important thing here is to sit in a way that you can be comfortable, yet present, for however long you choose to practice.

Same goes for hands. Many might recommend certain hand postures, called *mudras*. Some say to put your hands in your lap, some say on your knees. Just find what is comfortable and sustainable for you.

There are also different views about what to do with your eyes during meditation: Some traditions recommend sitting with your eyes open; others say closed. Some say eyes closed helps you turn inward; some say eyes open keeps you connected to both the outer and inner landscapes. Personally, I tend to practice with my eyes half open, because closed eyes often lead to daydreaming—or actual sleep! But again, just do whatever works for you.

Okay. *So.* You're sitting. You're somewhere quiet. You're comfortable yet attentive. Now what?

Well, now you breathe.

And then what?

Nothing! You *just* breathe.

Sometimes, you'll find that seems like an impossible task. Your mind will jump from thought to thought: *What did I do last night? What do I have to do today? Pizza or tacos for lunch? Do birds ever shit and it accidentally hits another bird mid-flight? And if so, do they have some kind of a bird wreck? I wonder if I can fit my fist into my mouth. . . .*

It's true: your mind is a wacky place and your thoughts *will* be all over the place. The important thing here is to begin to notice.

Take note when a thought pops up, then smile to your-self and do your best to let it go. It can sometimes help to note the thought by saying something like "thinking." It won't be long before another equally distracting thought pops up. That's okay, just keep noticing and returning to breathing. Noticing and returning: that's what med-itation *is.*

If you get discouraged, keep in mind that your mind has spent pretty much its entire existence thinking that it's in charge, so learning to let thoughts go without attaching to them is going to take some time. Just be patient and kind with yourself. I cannot stress enough the importance of self-kindness. Remember that, at your core, you're a good being and you're doing your best. And breathe.

Do this practice for as long as you find feels right. Perhaps a few minutes, perhaps even longer. You may find it helpful to set a timer and make a decision not to move until it goes off. Whether it's an hour, half an hour, or even five minutes a day, you will begin to notice it coming a bit easier after a while. You may very well find your mind starting to get quiet and your heart starting to open. Lit-tle by little, you will begin to even *feel* that you really are reconnecting with your true self. If there's one thing I hope you take from this book, it's to start sitting. For even five minutes a day, just sit.

tl;dr

Sit comfortably. Open or closed, keep your eyes relaxed. Sit and breathe, noticing your breath and also noticing when you're *not* noticing it. When you find yourself thinking instead of noticing, think, "thinking," and return your attention to your breath. Do this at least once a day, for at least five minutes a day. And if you can and want to manage more, do!

3.

Everything Sucks

Or, On Your Way to a Perfect Day!

SO. HERE WE ARE. You, me, and 7.4 billion other human beings. We're moving around on this earth, trying to live our lives, and maybe find some sort of happiness and meaning in them. We work, make friends, start families, and if we have spare time, find ways to pass that time. It all seems simple enough.

But something is wrong. It seems no matter how much energy we put into being happy, we find ourselves struggling through our days unable to achieve and maintain happiness. What's the problem here?

Even if everything seems perfect, you'll still find yourself wanting something more. You've got the dream job, the nice house, a couple of kids, and some free time to play around on your guitar. Maybe you even had sex today! But now what? Now, you're afraid of losing it all or desperate for some next new moment of happiness.

Your mind utterly fills itself with thoughts, many of them just completely awful: what could go wrong, what has gone wrong, what you wish were different. Your mind is racing, deliberating about a million things. But one thing *hasn't* crossed your mind: the truth. That is, the actual, bare-bones, free-from-any-perceptions, 100% undeniable truth—the truth of the present moment. You are disconnected. So you keep on living, confused, unhappy, always feeling that something is missing.

But let me throw this out there: what if, really, *nothing* is missing? Sounds a little batshit, I know—but consider it for a moment.

What if the truth is that you always have everything you need at any given moment, and even the seemingly shitty moments are actually perfect? What if the problem isn't one of circumstances but one of perspective? What if everything sucks only as much as you *believe* it sucks, and if you'd knock that shit off, everything wouldn't suck so much?

Example time: Let's say you're walking down the street. And let's say that's *all* we say about that. Pretty boring little story, isn't it? So let's start over with more information. Okay. Walking Down the Street, Take 2: You're walking down the street, your dog has just died, your significant other has left you, and you're on your way to a meeting at work where you're pretty sure you're going to get fired. *Now* how do you feel? Pretty shitty, right?

Now let's try a different scenario for Take 3: You're walking down the street again, but this time your dog is fine, your significant other and you are crazy in love, and you're pretty sure that meeting you're headed to is going to result in a big raise. How do you feel this time? Good, or even great, right? But hold on to your ass, because I'm about to suggest something that might not sit well at first: all three of these scenarios are kind of the same.

You might be thinking, "Get the fuck out of here, Miguel," and I wouldn't blame you, but hear me out.

It comes down to this: no matter what has happened before or will happen after, the only moment that actually exists is the present moment—the moment you're living right now.

After again telling me to get the fuck out, you might argue that the past is real. After all, you lived it, you remember it, you've got photos and everything. That all may be true, but the past is *the past*—it can never be lived again, and it's always going to be blurred by our imperfect memories and perceptions. Essentially, it's not real. It's really just an idea.

And as for the future, well . . . that might be even less real! No matter how much energy we spend thinking about the future or trying to make it a certain way, we can never really control the moment or experience it—until it has become the present.

Let's go back to Take 2 of our walking scenario, the version in which you're having a shitty day, and break it down:

The dog died, that's true. But in *this moment* the dog is not dying. In this moment you are simply walking. Your partner left you. Okay, that happened too, but in this moment you are simply walking. And yes, your boss might be *about* to tell you that you are the worst employee ever and fire your ass, but in this moment, you are (*say it with me now!*) simply walking. None of the stuff that has happened before is real *right now*. None of the stuff that may happen soon is real *right now*. The only real thing right now is the step you're taking and what's happening as you take it. If you can remember that, you can shift your attention to that one step, reconnecting to the present moment. When you reconnect like that, that's *peace.*

The same goes for Take 3: Your partner loves you, your dog is fine, your boss might even give you a proverbial blowjob and hand you a million-dollar bonus. But again, none of that is real. At least, not right now! Right now you are walking. That is the only real thing.

So the first scenario—the seemingly boring one where all you're doing is walking—is the only true one. Not only that, it is actually the best one: because if you are simply walking and you are fully mindful that that's what you're doing, then the past and the future live where they belong, and you live where you belong—here and now.

You can try a zillion times in life to escape the seemingly mundane present moment—we all do!—but that's a futile endeavor that pretty much only leads to more suffering. And that brings us back to the idea of perspective versus circumstance. We're not bored by the idea of simply walking because walking is boring. It's because we have become so disconnected that we've lost perspective. The fact is that being a human is an amazing opportunity that most creatures don't get to experience, and those who do only get to for a limited time. If we spend all our time living in fantasy—and that's what the past and future are, ultimately—we are probably missing the point.

If each new moment is the only moment we really have, how do we make the most of it? We take in what helps us reconnect, and we let go of what no longer serves us. It's a lesson our breath has been trying to show us our entire life: *take in, let go, repeat.*

It's a process that we can, and I think should, do over

and over again, day to day, year to year, for our entire life. Each day is waiting for us to let it be our perfect day.

But if you're hoping to find something in this book that will instantly obliterate all your problems, you're not going to find it. Reconnecting is a lifelong practice, a journey with no end. There's no shortcut through which—*boom!*— you're suddenly enlightened and have no more issues or emergencies or shitty-feeling days. In fact, many of those things that do seem to offer an immediate sense of satisfaction fade quickly, leaving us even less connected than before. This is why that extra slice of pizza, that new pair of running shoes, or that giant 3D TV will never fully make you happy. They might bring you a temporary distraction, but they don't offer an actual connection.

That's not to say there's anything wrong with eating that extra slice of pizza, or enjoying those new running shoes, or the TV. There isn't anything wrong with any of it. The problem comes when we allow these things to take us away from the present moment. If the present moment involves eating a slice of pizza, perfect, enjoy it—and then be willing to let it go. Once that moment is over, the pizza no longer serves you. And this point brings me to something we will revisit often in this book: letting go of what no longer serves you.

It seems like a simple enough concept: when something is getting in the way of your ability to reconnect, let it go. At some point it will be time for everything we know—things, people, places, events, and even ourselves—to move on. It may seem sad, but it's true. This is known as the truth of impermanence. We'll talk more about that later. For now, just start thinking more often about letting go. The more you can accept the idea of letting go, the more ease you'll find in your day-to-day life, and the closer you'll come to achieving a perfect day. Just remember that this "perfect day" isn't necessarily the sex-having, adventure-taking, everything-is-going-my-way day you might think it is.

Your perfect day is already happening now.

The question is whether or not you're connected to it.

■ ■ ■

Practice: Walk the Walk

Set aside some time for a walk. This can be ten minutes, it can be an hour—however long you think you can devote to simply walking. Leave your phone or any other distractions behind. Now decide where you're going to walk. Some might find it easier to walk in a circle around their living room; others might want to go outside for a nice stroll. Choose something that's going to work for you, but again, keep distractions to a minimum. If you're walking in your house, turn off the TV, let the dogs outside, and do anything else you can for quiet. If you're going outside, try to find a route where there aren't a ton of cars or people. Some might be unavoidable, but you probably want to avoid doing this practice, say, in Times Square.

Now that you've decided where you're going to walk and for how long . . .

1. Take an actual step. Walk slowly, mindfully. As you inhale, slowly lift your left foot off the ground, and then using your entire exhale, lower it down.

2. Repeat, but with your right foot.

3. Keep going, taking a full breath in and out with each

step. Try not to think too much; just simply note the sensation of breathing and of walking. How does your foot feel lifting off the earth? How does it feel stepping back down? How is your breath doing? As much as possible, let go of distracting thoughts and return to the very simple breath: in and out. Observe how bringing this attention to the seemingly simple act of walking can help you connect. There's nothing in this moment but the left foot stepping, then the right foot, then the left again. It might sound boring, and sometimes it may in fact be boring, but it's good for you. Give your mind a rest, and walk with a calm mind and an open heart. Know that there is nothing to do but breathe and walk. Simply enjoy your breathing and your walking.

tl;dr

Go take an undistracted walk. Breathe in as you lift your left foot up, breathe out as you set your left foot down. Repeat on the right foot. Continue walking and breathing. If at some point you realize you are still walking but not breathing, you may have died and come back like in a George Romero movie.

In that case, keep walking and find brains.

4.

On the Impossible Past

DISCONNECT is a real fucking problem: it's the single biggest obstacle between us and the truth. So we need to see it in all its forms—past, present, and future.

One good way to think of disconnection is as separation. When we're disconnected, we become separated from our authentic selves, from each other, and from the reality of the world around us. And, of course, we find ourselves separated from the present moment. But in reality the present moment is the only moment we have.

One of the many ways humans love to disconnect is by living in the past. We spend our days reliving our old "successes" and "failures" over and over and over again: *What if I had asked that girl out? Why did I eat so many tacos? Remember that one party where . . . ? That was the best! Why can't all of my life be like that?*

We can spend our whole lives replaying some moment from the past, and some of us do just that. But no matter how much mental energy we devote to it all, no one will ever find themselves magically transported back in time with a second chance to do things differently. In fact, all this repetitive thinking about the past is good for one thing and one thing only: robbing ourselves of the present moment.

There is, of course, value in acknowledging our mistakes and learning and growing from them. But we still need to avoid getting *stuck* in the past. A big part of this involves accepting that things are how they are and they can be no other way.

It's no exaggeration to say that every single thing that has ever happened had to happen for you to be here today as you are, or that every person who has lived before us and every event that has ever occurred have played some role in making this moment exist. Everything—good, bad, neutral—has played some role in why things are as they are today. We're connected with everything and everyone.

Let's take a look at an example. This one isn't cheery, but I promise you, it's important.

When I was sixteen, I lost my mother to cancer. She was fifty-one years old. One day I am just a punk kid riding my BMX bike around with my friends; next thing I know I have no mom. It was devastating to put it lightly.

And things were just getting started. Just seven months later I lost my sister, Ana Suin Chen, my only sibling, to a car accident. She was twenty years old. I didn't think I would survive these losses, one after another.

We'll get into more on both of these people, and both of those events, later. For now though, I just want to acknowledge their deaths so that we can begin to examine how the past works.

I owe my family everything. They taught me how to live, how to love, how to be human. If it were up to me, would my mom have died? Would I have lost my sister at such a young age? Of course not. I would still have a mom and a sister. Maybe I'd be an uncle by now. I could know that if the day comes for me to have kids, they would know and be loved by their grandmother and aunt.

But that's not reality. That's wishing for the past and present to be different and daydreaming of a future that can never exist. I refuse to spend my life denying the past or regretting how things are—and so should you. The past may seem alive in our minds and our hearts, but we still have to move forward. I'm not trying to be cold or harsh or tough. This is not "Everyone dies and who gives a shit anyway, so let's party." That's not truth. That's not connection.

The point is, no matter what has happened in the past, you can live with an open heart today. I repeat: *No matter what has happened, you can still live with an open heart.*

I STILL FIND MYSELF thinking about my mother and sister often, reflecting on how their lives and deaths have brought me to where I am today. I believe that's how we can all approach our pasts. Here are a few examples of how these particular events got me to where I am today.

After Mom and Ana died, I decided to drop out of high school. My father insisted that I finish, so I got my GED and started college early. Meanwhile I'd decided that if we're all going to die anyway and don't know when it's going to happen, then I may as well live how I want to live. So I kept playing music and eventually joined Teenage Bottlerocket. I was able to live my dreams, to play music I love with people I love, and to travel all over the world.

Had my mother and sister not died when and how they did, it's likely I would have finished high school, completed my bachelor's degree in four years instead of seven, gone on to get a master's, and landed a stable job—all in all, a much "safer" way of living. There's nothing wrong with that, but it was never what was in my heart.

My family, though, had always taught me to live from my heart, and their deaths had taught me that safety is an illusion. Without their deaths, without my past being the way it was, I couldn't be who I am today. And while that might seem tragic from some perspectives, it really is the only way things can be.

There's a very real beauty in allowing things to be as they are. I could sit and wish really, really hard for my mom and sister to still be alive, but that won't ever work. So instead I carry them with me every step of the way. I acknowledge and accept my past. I let go of what no longer serves me, and I carry my loved ones in my heart. I do this every day—and so can you, with yours. Accepting your past and moving forward will help you connect.

It's a way to transform what would otherwise be a burden into something truly liberating.

Another thing to remember about the past, especially as it relates to our quest for connection, is this: the past is never going to be exactly what we think it was.

Ever notice how two people who went through the exact same experience can remember it so differently? It's because our perceptions get in the way of the truth. There will always be jaded ideas, opinions, confusion, and just flat-out lies our brain has told us about the past. Your mind and ego, if you let them run freely, will even convince you the past is real. Don't fall for these tricks. Remind yourself: "I am here, and I am here *now*. There is no other place and no other time. No matter who I have been or what I've done in the past, that's not who I am today. And while in some real sense I am the product of everything that has ever happened, no single event or handful of events can define that. Today I am me. Things could only have ever happened the way they did. There is no other way."

It's our attitude toward these truths that will determine our connectedness and our happiness.

■　■　■

Practice: Letting Go

We'll be building on the basic meditation instructions from chapter 2, but before you sit down, find a pen and something to write on and set them within reach.

1. First, find a comfortable seated position and bring awareness to your breath. Sit and breathe, very simply, in ... and out. If you find yourself thinking about something else and not paying attention to your breath, gently note internally that you are in fact "thinking," and then allow the thought to go as you return to your breath. Do this for five, ten, thirty, forty-five minutes—however long works for you. In my experience how consistently you sit is more important than for how long. (If you've been practicing daily, you may find you are able to sit longer than before, or maybe you're not noticing that at all. Either way is totally fine, totally normal. Just keep sitting.)

2. Completing your planned breathing meditation time, draw your attention to your thoughts. Begin to

contemplate your past, and find one specific event or moment that you feel keeps you stuck. It is something from your past that you can't let go of.

3. Instead of running away from this difficult, sticky thought, sit with it for a few moments—even if it's really uncomfortable to do so. Notice how it feels to give attention to it.

4. Internally, offer yourself and the thought some compassion. Remember that the event you are focusing on was an important part of making you who you are today. Also know that it is time to let go, time to move forward. Absorb the lessons of the past, reflect on them, and take them in with an open heart. Then gently release, breathing out and giving yourself permission to move on.

5. Grab your pen and paper. Write down the event that has kept you from connecting to the present so many times. Use as much or as little detail as serves you today.

6. Once you've finished writing, take a moment to read what you have written. Breathe in and breathe out as you sit with whatever sensations come up. Then decide to let go.

7. Take the paper, and with a sense of gratitude—knowing the words there brought you to where you are today— fold the paper up. Fold it neatly or crumple it—doesn't matter. Now stand up. Take the note, and throw it away. Let yourself rest in the relief of the moment.

tl;dr

After sitting in meditation, write down something you've been holding on to, something that keeps you from moving forward. Give yourself permission to accept the lesson and to let go. Take that piece of paper, crumple it up, throw it away, light it on fire, take a piss on it—whatever you need to do to really leave it behind.

5.

The Future Ain't What It Used to Be

IF THE PAST DOESN'T EXIST and can't be changed, and we can't recall how it really was anyway, we should focus on the future, right? Wrong. Why? Because the future doesn't exist either. Not yet at least. And even if we spend time and energy anticipating the future, it will never turn out to be what we expect it to be. Honestly, it's better that way. So we should focus our energy on the here and now.

The modern Zen-inspired philosopher Alan Watts said something about rich people that, in a way, applies to most of us here in the West: that they "understand much more about making and saving money than about using and enjoying it. They fail to live because they are always preparing to live." Wealthy or not, we all dream of bright futures, big rewards, and a day when—later—we will finally have the life we want.

Of course there's nothing wrong with thinking about tomorrow. It's incredibly valuable, for example, for each of us to keep the health and future of our planet in our minds. But we won't ever truly have an effect on the future unless we are living here and now. And our ideas about the future have just as much potential to cause a disconnect as those about the past. For example, if we're afraid the government is going to try to build an impossibly expensive and ineffective wall to keep out an imaginary threat, well, we might be right. But sitting around worrying about it isn't doing any good.

We've been living for the future our entire lives: When we're kids, we can't wait to be teenagers. When we're teenagers, we can't wait to be in our twenties. When we're in our twenties, we begin to think maybe we should consider buying a home, getting married, starting a family. When we're in our thirties, we might find ourselves stuck somewhere between worrying about the future and longing for the past. I haven't hit my forties yet, but it seems the people I know who have worry just as much about the future as younger folks.

We sit, we long for the future, we make plans. We have all of these ideas about how things are going to be and how we are going to feel, what it's going to be like when we finally get "there." But we're never going to get "there." The future is never going to be how you imagine it will be, so why spend your life imagining? You are already *here*.

Sure, "here" might suck in a "extreme bigots have been empowered to walk around in the open for the first time in decades" kind of way. But, with the right perspective, we can deal with and even benefit from even that. Now that they're out in the open we can more efficiently fight to overcome bigotry and hatred. And maybe, just maybe, we can make contact with some of them and show them a better way.

At my studio, Blossom Yoga in Laramie, we spend a lot of time working on being here and letting go of the future. A common saying in the spiritual community, and at Blossom, is "Do your best and let go of the results." (I like to think of it as "Do your best, fuck the rest.") This means that the work we do now is what's important. What becomes of it is, at least right now, not so important, because the future doesn't exist. The present moment is the only moment in which we can actually find connection. It's the only moment that exists.

There are a million examples of how focusing on the future robs us, but I'd like to start with one that's near and dear to so many of our hearts:

Sex!

Let's say you've found a partner who consensually wants to get down with you. You've spent hours or days or months or years or however long building up to this moment. Now here you are. Your naughty parts, their naughty parts. Awesome, right? You get stoked thinking about how good it's gonna feel when you, um . . . finish. In fact, you get so stoked you make it all about you. Your partner is bummed, you missed the entire experience, and now you're just sitting there with a mess to clean up. Bummer. You start the cycle over again, swearing up and down that next time it'll be better.

Let's try this scenario again, only this time, you're not worried about the future. This time you stay present. So you and your hot date have reached that point. It's time to do it. Fuck yeah. You start kissing. Awesome. You start touching each other. Awesome. You take your time, you enjoy the process, you make love. You have an experience that lasts minutes or hours or however long it's supposed to last, but you don't worry about time—because you are here, in the moment. You're not performing. You're having *a real human experience.*

When the time comes to finish, you do just that, and it is especially awesome. Your partner and you clean up, cuddle for a while, and then go get tacos. High-five!

See the difference?

HERE'S ANOTHER GOOD, if not quite as sexy, example. Let's say you know you want to make good money, buy a house, get married, and start a family. You spend your entire life prepping for the day you will finally have everything you want.

You go to college, work your ass off, get good grades, and get your degree. Along the way, a number of your relationships struggle and even fall away, because you are so focused on your goal. That's okay though, you've got somewhere to go. You find a job, work hard, start making some money.

In time, you do in fact meet someone, get serious, and kids become part of the picture. It seems you're well on your way to reaching your goal. Your many hours at the office keep you away from your family, but they understand you are just trying to give them everything they need.

You work, and work, and work, always keeping your eye on the prize. Then one day you're driving home and get killed in an accident. No warning, no heads-up, just dead.

The future you worked so hard for is a total nonoption in an instant. Your family is left behind without you. That part is certainly tragic, but also inevitable. (We are all going to die and we never know when, so accepting death has to become a part of our journey. We'll talk more on that later. For now let's accept the "fact" that you died.) But Alan Watts would see the other real tragedy here: you never really lived. You were so dedicated to the illusion of the future, you passed up the only thing you really had, the present.

A grim example, but its lesson is very freeing: if tomorrow might not come, then all we ever truly need to do is our best today. *Do your best and let go of the results.*

One more thing: just because the tomorrow we imagine might not ever come doesn't give us license to live like idiots. If anything, it means we should be even more present. If this were your last day alive, would you really want to spend it in a drunken haze puking all over yourself? Or would you rather be connected, with a calm mind and an open heart, at peace?

(Incidentally, if you do happen to be in a drunken haze puking all over yourself, no need to punish yourself about it. I've been there. I might be there again. That's what this moment entails, and a new one is coming soon. In the meantime, clean yourself up and drink some water.)Today is all we really have. So please, my friend, try this practice that will help you make the most of it.

■   ■   ■

Practice: Simple Yoga Poses

Some in the West still think of yoga as being just about people tying themselves into pretzels or standing on their head. We'll talk about yoga some more in later chapters, but for now let's leave it at this: it has a lot less to do with whether or not you can touch your toes, and a lot more to do with getting in touch with yourself. Yoga is often a lesson in letting go of the past or the future and finding yourself in the present moment. It is a practice of accepting yourself as you are here and now. So let's try some very simple yoga poses.

1. First, stand up nice and tall. Take your feet hip distance apart or closer. Release your hands to your sides, and flip your palms to face forward. This is *mountain pose.*

2. Here in mountain pose, take a moment to press into all four corners of both of your feet. Tuck in slightly through your navel, and down slightly through your tailbone. Now relax your shoulders down away from your ears. There you go. You're doing yoga.

3. From mountain pose, inhale, bring both arms up overhead, palms facing each other. Press the feet into the earth so the fingers can extend skyward. This is *extended* mountain pose. As you exhale, lead with your heart, bend at the waist, and "dive" forward, allowing the upper body to hang over the legs. This is a standing forward fold.

> *Note*: Many people think they need to get their hands to their toes in standing forward fold. It's perfectly fine if you can't. It's all okay! Let go of what you think the pose should look like; just feel it now.
>
> Here are a few tips for your forward fold. Take a deep bend in your knees. Often people think this pose is about keeping the legs straight and getting your fingers to touch the ground. That's not it. This is about the present moment. So allow yourself to bend through both knees. See how that shifts the stretch out of the legs and allows you to lengthen through your spine. Okay, let's get back to our instructions. We left off at your actually doing a standing forward fold.

4. You're still in standing forward fold. How does it feel? Give yourself permission to experiment with the pose,

to arrive in the present moment. Shake your head out—as in *yes* and *no*. Grab opposite elbows and gently sway from side to side. Straighten one leg, then the other. Find stillness. Know that wherever you are today is exactly where you are supposed to be. However this pose feels isn't good or bad, it simply is. Be here, now. Don't worry about what this pose might look like for you in the future; just enjoy a few moments being present in your body.

5. When you are finished, slowly roll back up to standing, stacking one vertebra at a time.

tl;dr

Find mountain pose. Inhale the arms up overhead, then exhale and fold over the legs. Take several moments in this forward fold to be present with yourself. Don't worry about the future. Don't worry about whether your hands touch your toes, or if they ever will. Simply allow yourself to be.

6.

Your Perfect Day

WHAT IS LIFE? *What is its meaning? What in the fuck are we doing here anyway?*

Humans have been asking questions like these for pretty much as long as we have been around. Some have gone insane in the search for the answer. So let's simplify.

For me, it helps to think of the meaning of life as this: *life is to be lived.*

We've seen that there is no past. We've seen that there is no future. So if life is to be lived, we must do it now.

Today is our day. Let's live it. What would *your* perfect day look like?

Perhaps it's something along the lines of *no work, sun is out, food is awesome, I get to party with all my friends and family, and responsibilities are out the door.* Or maybe your perfect day looks like this: *I get to sleep in as long as I want, be left alone, watch my favorite movie, and eat ice cream.*

Forget all that. In either case, it might *sound like* a perfect day, but it's not real and it doesn't come from the real you. It's mostly fantasy and delusion, and fantasies and delusions come from ego, which is what keeps you disconnected. The real you, the you that comes before all the fantasies and delusions crop up, knows that today—no matter what happens—really can be a perfect and meaningful day. Let's take a deeper look. It's Choose-Your-Own-Adventure time!

First, let's say a doctor has informed you that you're going to die tomorrow. If you're going to live a perfect day, there's no two ways about it: it has to be today. You start things off by calling work and telling them to kindly shove the job up their ass. Next, you tell all your friends that it's your last day to live and that you need to party. Then, you do just that. You eat all your favorite foods, go to all your favorite places, get drunk off your ass. It is truly the party of a lifetime. You head home to crash.

What happens next? (Spoiler alert: it won't be quite as fun as the rest of the day has been.)

Scenario 1: You get another call from the doctor. Seems they messed up—you're not actually dying. *Whoops!* It sounds like great news, but your past hours of excess have caused some major problems: For starters, you don't have a job anymore. Also, you're *super* hung-over and have spent the whole day pretty much eating garbage. A lot of your so-called perfect day has been spent between bed and the toilet.

Scenario 2: The sun rises the next morning, but you don't: you never wake up. It actually *was* your last day. And yeah, you spent it partying, but you were so wasted and disconnected, you hardly noticed much about it, and let's just say that your affairs are definitely not in order. Now you're gone.

Either way, it was not much of an adventure. Luckily, though, you can make a better choice earlier on.

You see, every moment of every day is a new opportunity. We can use these moments to connect or to disconnect. It's our level of connection that makes the difference between a perfect day and a shitty one, and it's all up to us.

Consider what makes up an "average" day for so many of us: You wake up to an alarm, drag yourself out of bed, make some coffee, and head straight to work, where you mostly just numb your mind, get your shit done, scroll through Facebook, and wait for the day to be over. Then you head home, pick up something to eat, sit down, watch TV, and fall asleep. The next day you do the same thing. And you do this for days and weeks and months and years.

It happens all of the time.

Well, fuck that.

Even if your day *does* revolve around waking up, going to work, heading home, and then going to bed, there is still plenty of room for connection and beauty. You have the power to take your seemingly ordinary days and transform them into perfect ones. Let's think through the same seemingly mundane day, but this time imagining living with a wide open heart:

You wake up and take a moment to acknowledge the unlimited potential of the day ahead of you. You know you're lucky to be alive. You make coffee and a little breakfast, and even if you have to finish it on the way to work, you still take care to notice and appreciate the flavors and the nourishment.

The job really does make you unhappy, so you use your breaks to actively look—not just pretend to look—for something else to do with your life. You can't quite up and leave today, but you have taken an important first step, and there's relief in knowing that you're taking control. At the end of the day you head home, enjoying music along the way. You come home, cook yourself a good dinner, notice the flavor in each bite, and even find a moment of appreciation while washing the dishes: you are alive, you are well, and you have much to be grateful for.

Things may not be perfect, but when you stop thinking about living and start doing it instead, you're on your way to a perfect day. Life, after all, is to be lived.

If not today, then when?

■ ■ ■

Practice: Sun Salutation A (Modified)

Let's build on the basic yoga we tried out in the last chapter. To recap: Mountain pose is standing up straight. Extended mountain pose is the same pose with the arms overhead. Then we have a forward fold. Together these are about half of the postures that make up a basic sun salutation. Sun salutation is a very simple flow of postures, which helps us wake up the body, connect to our breath, and welcome the day ahead. There are variations depending on who is teaching you or what style of yoga you are doing, but what we'll try now is a very basic, very safe version. Let's learn the whole thing.

1. Begin standing in mountain pose. Inhale, bringing your arms up overhead for extended mountain pose.

2. Exhale, leading with your heart as you fold over your legs into the standing forward fold.

3. Inhale to rise partway into a half lift with the hands on the shins and the back flat.

4. Exhale to fold back forward. This time, plant your hands on the ground and step your feet back into a high plank, or the "top" of a pushup.

5. Inhale here in your plank, and then as you exhale, hug in your elbows as you lower your body closer to your mat (this pose is a low plank). Now lower your body all the way to your mat. Untuck your toes, press the tops of your feet down, and press your hands down, inhaling to gently lift your chest up off the mat coming into cobra pose. You're looking for a light back bend here, with the crown of the head extended long and the shoulder blades drawn together. Lower your chest back down, and come flat on your belly as you exhale.

6. Then tuck your toes back onto the mat, draw your navel in, and inhale to push back up into your high plank. From here you will exhale as you lift your hips up and back while you push through your arms to come into downward-facing dog. Here you want to spread wide through the fingers, press the palms down, lengthening the spine and pushing sits bones to the sky, while pressing heels down toward the earth.

> *Note*: Often you'll see people doing downward-facing dog, pressing their heels down "into the earth," or floor. You might find that your heels are nowhere near the floor. That's totally fine. It's not about how you look in the pose but how it feels in the body. Your heels may never touch the floor because, for example, of the way your body is built. Or maybe they will. Either way it's the same pose. If it helps you find length in your spine, bend through your knees.

7. From down dog (which is short for "downward-facing dog"), inhale as you lift the head and look at the top of your mat, and exhale as you step your feet forward between your hands, coming back to your standing forward fold.

8. Inhale as you lift your torso halfway, bringing your hands to your shins, exhale to fold back down. Inhale again as you rise all the way up to extended mountain pose. Exhale, releasing your hands down to your side, palms facing forward as you come into mountain pose.

That's it. That's sun salutation A! You'll find the whole sequence illustrated for you on pages 46–47.

It's a simple flow that you can practice on your own and will encounter often in many yoga classes. Try doing one, or many. I have a friend who does 108 in a row to welcome a new month—don't do that unless you really, really want to.

The most important thing to remember while doing your sun salutation is to breathe.

Connecting breath to motion will help ground you in the moment and clear space for the day ahead. Today is an awesome day, full of opportunities. Let's greet it accordingly!

tl;dr

Start in mountain pose. (See pages 46–47.)

Inhale as you lift the arms to the sky, coming into extended mountain pose.

Exhale as you hinge at the hips, coming into forward fold.

Inhale to rise up halfway, bringing the hands to shins or thighs.

Exhale to fold forward. Bring the hands to plant on the mat.

Inhale as you step both feet back to a high pushup position.

Exhale as you lower all the way down onto the belly.

Untuck the toes, inhale as you press hands down, and gently lift the chest into cobra pose. Exhale to lower onto the belly. Tuck the toes, inhale, and push back into a high plank pose. Exhale to send the hips up and back for downward-facing dog.

Inhale to lift the gaze and look at the top of the mat.

Exhale and walk the feet to in between the hands, coming to forward fold.

Inhale to rise up halfway, finding a flat back.

Exhale to fold forward.

Inhale, come to standing, and reach the arms overhead for extended mountain pose.

Exhale, release the hands by the sides, and return to mountain pose.

Repeat as many times as you'd like.

7.

Wake Up

YOUR ALARM GOES OFF, and your first thought
is something along the lines of "Oh, shit." You're still so
tired. You can't believe you have to get up, much less get up
and "go get 'em." And for what? It's just another cycle of
sleeping, shitting, and even more time at work—or school,
or just . . . life.

Sound familiar? Of course it does. We've all been there,
or someplace like it. It's easy for us to get stuck in these
seemingly endless cycles, easy for us to assume that things
aren't going to go our way, that today is going to suck or
be mediocre at best.

But have you ever noticed that the more attention you
give to such ideas, the more they seem to come true? That's
because your thoughts and your overall attitude really do
help determine the quality of your days and your very life.

That's good news, because—while you may not believe
it yet—you're ultimately the one in control. You have the
power to train your mind so that not even the worst drudg-
ery of life will be able to pull you down. With the right
frame of mind you can reconnect, again and again, to your
authentic self. The more you do it, the more your heart
opens, and that helps you navigate life with less stress
and suffering.

There's a term for that right frame of mind, one that's recognized by both punk rockers and more classically self-help spiritual-seeker types: "PMA" or positive mental attitude. It was the classic DC band Bad Brains who clued me and my friends in to PMA. Their song "Attitude" nailed the concept with its proud, defiant lyrics:

Don't care what they may do
We got that attitude
Don't care what they may say
We got that attitude
Hey!
We got that PMA!

What a beautiful sentiment. Whoever "they" are, it doesn't matter what they do; it only matters how you react to it. And we all get to choose our reactions, because we all get to choose our attitude. To me, that's very punk rock—way more than having green hair, putting safety pins through your face, or obsessively listening to the Ramones (all things I do or have done, by the way).

But the power of a positive mental attitude doesn't just apply to punk rockers. In fact, since punk is often associated with things like anti-capitalism, the DIY movement, and people-first politics, it might surprise you to learn that Bad Brains actually got the idea from a book by a guy named Napoleon Hill titled *Think and Grow Rich*.

That book is all about how the power of your attitude can shape everything in your life. Want to get rich? Then set your mind to it, Hill said, and you will succeed. But his book and the philosophy underlying it go much deeper than just monetary wealth. He understood how attitude can shape our entire existence, and so it's of universal value—even if money's the furthest thing from your mind.

The basic premise, in a way, is that life is what you make of it. That's a cliché, for sure, but that doesn't make it untrue. And I'll bet your own experience backs that up. Think of a time when you had to do something you didn't want to do and were sure you couldn't do anyhow. Maybe it was algebra homework, or writing a song, or doing twenty pushups. How'd it go? Bad, right? Right—because, if you don't believe you can succeed at something, you usually won't. Likewise, if you've got a shitty attitude about life, you're pretty much guaranteeing yourself a shitty life.

Working to keep an open heart and a positive attitude changes all that. Suddenly, there is no predetermined limit to what you can accomplish. Whatever the day brings, you can face it. And even if you wake up thinking "Oh, shit" yet again, so what? You still have the power and the opportunity to choose to go with PMA—not just when you get up, but hundreds, even thousands, of times throughout each new day. It's you who'll determine the quality of those days, and ultimately your life.

Cliché or not, it's all true, and it always has been. That's why so many ancient approaches to PMA are still practiced today, with essentially no changes.

Ayurveda is a good example. An ancient health system from India, it's still practiced by many and particularly popular among certain groups of yogis (practitioners of yoga or meditation). Essentially, the ayurvedic approach recognizes that there are different types of people and explains how each type can best live a balanced, healthy life. The system says we are all born "in balance" and that our problems come about when we fall out of balance.

Ayurveda gives us very detailed instructions on what we should do, and when, to achieve our supposed "ideal" balance: what types of food to eat, which exercises to do, when to go to the bathroom, when to nap. It's all based on your "type."

Now, I don't know that all of Ayurveda appeals to me or that it would to many of you. But I have found certain elements of it helpful, like the daily routine known as Dinacharya. It begins something like this:

- Wake up before the sun.

- Acknowledge the divine nature of life.

- Drink water.

- Take a shit.

- Clean yourself.

- Do yoga.

- Meditate.

- Live your life.

This is of course a *very* loose interpretation! And there are many wonderful books and teachers specializing in Ayurveda or Dinacharya, should you want to really study and go deep with them. But for now, let's just look at these first steps and how following them can help us wake up right and have not just a good day but a perfect one.

I don't know that you need to wake up before the sun, so don't if you don't want to. There are persuasive arguments for why you should; but if it's not realistic or is just unappealing, remember, this is about you, so do what you can do and live how you want to live! Back to the other steps.

Some of them are no-brainers. You definitely need to take a dump, because you're a living being. You may as well do that in the morning so you're not, um, carrying around extra shit. Also, water is important. (*Duh.*) It makes sense to start the day by drinking some. And don't be gross. Clean yourself.

Like I said, all obvious stuff. And while I'll get to meditation and yoga later, for now I want to talk about step two: acknowledge the divinity of life.

Yes, I know: that sounds a little "woo-woo." (OK: a *lot* woo-woo.) I mean, what exactly does it mean to "acknowledge the divinity of life"?

Well, it can mean anything you want it to, but basically, it's about starting the day with PMA. For some, that might mean stopping to thank God or some other higher power for another day on the planet. But for those who don't resonate with that kind of idea, it can simply mean really thinking, "I am happy to be here."

And you *should* be happy to be here—even on the worst days. I know it seems sometimes like the whole world is against us, nothing is going our way, and it sucks to be alive. But that's all an illusion. The fact is, it's pretty fucking amazing that we're here at all.

Think for a moment about every single thing that ever had to happen for you to be here today. You can't even. It's overwhelming. It's endless, nothing short of a miracle. So even when things don't go our way, even when we experience very real pain, we are still alive. And that is an amazing, even rare, thing to be. If we lose our appreciation of that, that's a major cause of disconnect. But we can always come back, we can always reconnect. That's our practice.

When we begin the day with appreciation, we're setting the tone for whatever comes next. It's a process of training and retraining our mind in a way that brings us away from disconnect and back to our true self, the part of us that knows how amazing it is to be alive, that every day offers us new opportunities and experiences. That's not something we should take for granted—but usually, we do exactly that.

When we think differently, we live differently. A simple shift in attitude can, for example, help us be more awake, alert, and ready for the day. If you *think* energetically, you *will* have an easier time getting up. So, what if, instead of "Oh, shit," you woke up with a sense of gratitude that you'd gotten some rest? Or simply that you were still alive? What if you started your day with PMA?

Easier said than done? Maybe. But then again, maybe not. It's time to try it and see for yourself.

■ ■ ■

Practice: Grateful for Another Day

Our practice for this chapter is a simple but effective one.

1. First, you'll want to come up with a short phrase that expresses an attitude of appreciation for another day of life. (Don't worry if you're not feeling it; that'll come later.) Your phrase should acknowledge the divinity or the awesomeness of life. For some, the actual phrase "Acknowledging the divinity of life" may work. For others, a simple "Thank you" will do. Perhaps "I am grate-

ful for another day, another chance" or even "Let's do this!" fits you better. It can be anything, though I find a short and simple phrase works best. It just has to resonate with you.

2. Once you have your phrase, begin practicing saying it to yourself every morning. Maybe write it on a sticky note that you put near your bed or even on your alarm clock. It can be hard to remember to recite your phrase first thing in the morning, especially if you've never tried anything like this before. But don't worry—over time it will become habit, and you'll be saying your phrase upon waking up quite naturally.

3. Stick with it. Observe how saying your simple phrase actually helps you start the day with a different attitude. See how training your mind in this way helps you go into your day more open to what life brings. When you wake up with appreciation, every new day is another beautiful one, and it's you who chose to make it that way.

tl;dr

Find a short phrase of gratitude. Say it to yourself first thing in the morning. Repeat every day!

8.

Breathe

OUR PERFECT DAY ALWAYS STARTS NOW, and it always starts with our very next breath—the most basic and profoundly powerful tool we have. We're all born with it, we all die without it, and it's with us for each step we take.

Our breath is such a constant factor in our lives, in fact, that we usually take it for granted. But—in addition to keeping us alive—the breath offers us the chance to connect over and over, moment after moment, *if* we *don't* take it for granted.

The diaphragm is both a voluntary and involuntary muscle. That means that we'll keep breathing even if we forget to. This is important: we get to live. (*Duh.*) But it's the voluntary aspect of the breath that allows us to go deeper than just merely breathing. Our capacity to control how quickly or slowly we breathe and to be mindful of our breathing gives us a powerful tool, one we can use right up until the moment we die.

Naturally, that's why so many spiritual (and nonspiritual) practices rely on the breath. If you're doing heavy exercise, using breath control can help you power through. In vinyasa yoga, you feel the power of linking your breath and your movement. In meditation, we sit and we breathe.

Connecting to the breath, being mindful of it, helps us connect to ourselves, calm our minds, and open our hearts.

Remember being a little kid, and how when you got all wound up some adult would tell you to stop and count to ten? That was all about breathing. They knew if you took a moment to pause and reconnect with your breath, you would likely act like less of an asshole. The same idea applies now that you're older too—and to just about any level of asshole-ness.

I spent a lot of my adolescence and early adulthood in and out of shrinks' offices and on and off meds. Diagnosed as bipolar, I experienced intense ups and downs: I might find myself so wound up in anxiety that I could barely function and later be crippled by depression. It's something I still work with today.

Back then, I relied on counselors and psychologists, but they could do only so much. The drugs they prescribed me left me feeling empty, and there were no other real solutions being offered. But I did find something that mitigated my anxiety and depression eventually: I learned to breathe. Here's why it worked.

Our minds provide us with a constant flow of thoughts. Some of these are useful and help keep us alive. Like if your mind is telling you not to put a fork in an electric socket, you should definitely listen, because you want to live.

Other thoughts are not as useful, and some of them just fill up time and space. Like *who wins: a T-Rex with a bazooka or a monkey with a knife?* Such a ridiculous question. (It's obviously the monkey. The T-Rex's tiny arms can't hold, aim, and fire a bazooka!)

Still other thoughts are just torturous. Like *I am unlovable* or *I'm literally the dumbest person to ever walk the earth.* Thoughts like these are just as absurd as the one about the monkey and the T-Rex, but harmful to us too. Sometimes, though, such thoughts enter our minds, and for whatever reason, we start to accept and identify with them. These torturous thoughts start to seem real to us.

Therein lies the problem. The mind, the ego, really wants to be in charge and will try all it can to convince you that it is. It will play out an infinite number of scenarios, send a million thoughts an hour your way, all to keep itself active and in the forefront of each moment. The ego will distract you from the present moment again and again to maintain the illusion that it is boss. Your breath, though, can help put it back in its place. As I've suggested earlier in this book (and will later too), *you are more than your mind.* Don't get me wrong: your mind is incredible, and incredibly valuable. It has saved your life, I guarantee, many times. But that doesn't mean you have to take any shit from it.

Whether it's your mind or some troubled asshole that's telling you something like "you are a total fucking idiot," in neither case is it true. You're *not* a total fucking idiot, even if you've done totally fucking idiotic things. Doing idiotic things is just part of the "being a human being" deal. And since attaching to these thoughts has never done you any good and never will, it's time to learn to let them go. How? You guessed it: breathe!

And as for the "filler" thoughts? They may be sort of harmless, but they aren't helping either. They're distractions, keeping you from connecting and appreciating whatever is actually in front of you. (Even if whatever's in front of you seems mind-numbingly boring, there's probably *something* of value there.) We can start letting go of these filler thoughts too by returning to the breath.

So whenever life seems overwhelming or you just need a rest from your thoughts, stop and breathe. It works. Love your mind for taking care of you, for keeping you alive, even for entertaining you. But when it's time to let thoughts go, stop, breathe, and rest in the here and now.

Written on my mother's grave is *si vivimos como respiramos, aspirando y dejando ir, no nos podemos equivocar.* That translates to *if we live like we breathe, taking in and letting go, we can't go wrong.*

■ ■ ■

Practice: Three-Part Breath

Yoga is more than physical practice—in fact, it's considered to have eight "limbs," and asana (taking and holding yoga postures) is just one of them. Also among the eight limbs of yoga you will find *pranayama*, or breath control. *Prana* is often thought of as the life force and is, unsurprisingly, related to the breath. So learning to control your breath is about connecting with your life force. In vinyasa yoga, which I teach a lot, movements are linked to breath. So, for example, you'll breathe in and put your arms up over your head.

There's a joke that the difference between doing yoga and just exercising is remembering to breathe. There are of course many other differences, because yoga is a lot more than just moving your body, but the importance of the breath here shouldn't be overlooked. Bringing attention to the breath can help us calm our minds and connect, so I often start my classes with a few minutes of breathing techniques. One of those techniques that I have found to be particularly useful is called three-part breath.

Before starting, find a quiet space and sit comfortably with your eyes either half-open or completely closed. Let your spine be tall but relaxed. Allow your hands to rest wherever is comfortable. Now bring awareness to your breath.

1. Follow the air as it moves in through your nose, expands softly into your lower belly, then moves back out the nose. This is the first part of the three-part breath. Again: in through the nose, into the belly, out through the nose. Stay with this for several breath cycles.

2. The second part of three-part breath builds on what you've done so far. Keep breathing in and out of the nose. Follow the air as it softens into the belly, then allow it to expand into the rib cage. As you exhale, do so first from the ribs, then belly, then out the nose. Stay with this for several slow, full-breath cycles.

3. Part three builds one more time on the foundation we've established. Breathe in through your nose into the belly, then the ribs, and then expand your sense of the presence of the air all the way up into your collarbones. The feeling in this third stage will be a bit subtler than in the other two. As you exhale, empty the air from your collarbone area, ribs, belly, and then nose. Stay here for several slow, full-breath cycles.

Three-part breath is said to be a grounding, healing breath. What do you think? How do you feel after a few minutes of it? I find it helps me calm down, quiet my mind, and arrive wherever I'm at. Your experience might be different, which is totally fine. The important part is that you made and took some time to be with your breath.

tl;dr

Sit down. Breathe in through your nose, into your belly, out your nose for a few cycles. Then add a few cycles of breathing in through your nose, into your belly, up into the ribs. Release ribs, belly, nose. Add one final cycle of breath in through your nose, belly, ribs, and into your collarbones. Then release collarbones, ribs, belly, nose.

9.

I Wanna Be Well

HAVING SPENT YEARS FIGHTING depression and anxiety, I have experienced firsthand the harm that comes from a lack of self-love. The thoughts of a depressed person can be straight-up evil: *I'm not good enough. I will never be good enough. I'm a giant fuckup. This world would be better off without me. All I do is cause problems. I deserve to suffer.*

Strong as they may seem sometimes, thoughts like these don't have any value. They just keep us in a cycle of self-hate and self-pity and disconnection. You most definitely deserve better.

The reality is that you are your one and only constant companion in this life. You are stuck with yourself. So if you want to be happy, you're going to need to learn how to get along with yourself and not be your own enemy. You need to develop self-love.

In my own journey, modern psychology and medicine may have temporarily alleviated some symptoms of self-hate, but they didn't really address the root of my problems. Sometimes, they even made things worse: on several occasions I've been prescribed drugs that not only didn't help me, but instead led me to further disconnect. Things seemed to change when I put the prescriptions down and spent time cultivating my relationship to myself. (Please note that I'm not saying that prescribed medications can't help people. If they prove to help you, you should stick with them. Just make sure, as always, that you are working toward a better connection with yourself rather than moving further away from self-love.)

It turns out that having a connection with yourself can feel a bit uncomfortable at first, especially if you've spent most of your life believing terrible things about yourself. The good thing is that if you spend time really getting to know yourself, you'll soon see yourself as you really are. You'll see that you're not bad. You're one of a kind even.

You are the only *you* that will ever exist. No one else will ever live the life you live, with the ups and downs, the challenges and advantages, the love and loss you will face. No one else can offer the world what you can. This makes you a gift to this world, and to yourself.

If your mind tries to convince you otherwise, remember this: you are not your thoughts. Your mind is a tool to help you get through this world, but it is not all of who you are. If your thoughts aren't helping you live fully, they are not serving you. Work to let them go and to instead cultivate ones that nurture you and help you move forward.

Sounds like a bunch of hippie talk, right? That may be so, but it's true. The point is, you need to be kind and appreciate yourself. So here's a practice to help you do just that.

■ ■ ■

Practice: Metta

In Buddhism, there is a practice called *metta*, or loving-kindness meditation. It involves sitting and "sending" a sense of open friendliness and warmth to yourself and others. For this chapter we will focus only on the first part. After all, you can't be much help to others if you can't find peace with yourself!

Remember how, in the practice from chapter 2, I said we'd be using basic meditation as a foundation for many of the practices in this book? Yep. Here we go again!

1. Sit comfortably—on the floor, on a cushion, in a chair; whatever posture you can sustain for a while. Find a tall, but not rigid, spine. Soften your gaze or close your eyes completely.

2. Bring awareness to your breath. Breathe in. Breathe out. If your mind begins to wander, gently draw it back to your breath. Allow your mind to settle and your heart to begin to open. Stay with this for several minutes.

3. Now, with a calmer mind and an open heart, begin to envision yourself. This can be any image of yourself for which it's easy to send kindness. It might be you as you are today. Maybe it's you as a small child, or even an infant. Perhaps this vision of yourself is in the distant future. Whatever version of yourself you imagine, hold it in your mind's eye, considering that this version of yourself is unique, being a culmination of everything that ever happened before, and that it has so many gifts to offer.

4. Now you'll begin to cultivate a sense of loving-kindness, or metta. This sense grows from a place of compassion in you, a place that (whether you're normally in touch with it or not) wants to feel and give love. It's a very

real, true part of you, as it is in us all. You really can touch in to it.

5. Once you start to feel connected with and rooted in this feeling of loving-kindness, begin to offer it to the image of yourself that you've conjured. Breathing in, say to yourself, *May I be well*. Note that being "well" doesn't mean we will never feel pain, get sick, or feel bad again. It simply means we will be able to handle whatever we are facing.

6. Sit with this for a few moments. Note how it feels to send yourself this kindness. Maybe it feels natural or maybe quite foreign. You might find yourself accepting or resisting. Either way is fine. Simply note your reaction, and sit with it.

7. Repeat the phrase, *May I be well*. Feel your edges softening, know that whatever emotions you feel are valuable. Allow them to transform into loving-kindness. Again: *May I be well*. Sit here for a few moments. Allow your heart to open. One more time: *May I be well*.

8. Gently let go of any words or thoughts that come up, returning to the very simple breath. *In. Out.* There is nothing left to do here but breathe and absorb the benefits of the practice.

9. After a few moments, allow your eyes to gently flutter back open. Bring some small movement back into your body. Wiggle your fingers and toes.

10. When you are ready, stand up, and walk into your day. Carry your sense of kindness with you. At any point during the day if you catch yourself being harsh toward

yourself, stop. Take a breath in and repeat: *May I be well.* Try to keep a calm mind and an open heart, and know you can handle whatever the day may bring.

tl;dr

Sit and breathe. After several moments begin to picture yourself. As you hold an image of yourself, begin to send it loving-kindness. Breathing in, say quietly to yourself, *May I be well.* Sit with that for several moments. Repeat: *May I be well.* Do this two more times. After several moments, return to your body and to your day, carrying this kindness with you throughout. If you find yourself being harsh toward yourself, take a moment, breathe in, and repeat: *May I be well.*

10.

Together Again for the First Time

CHECK OUT THAT ASSHOLE OVER THERE.

You might think you and that guy have absolutely nothing in common, and you might be right—on the surface, anyway. But if you stop and take a closer look, you'll realize that you're actually a lot alike.

No, I'm not calling *you* an asshole. What I mean is, everyone—and I mean *everyone*—has a life, and even if it looks nothing like your own, it's still every single bit as complicated and every single bit as valid. And yet, it's easy to look at the whole world with a "me-versus-them" mentality.

That mentality keeps us disconnected—and not just a little. It's at the root of why wars are fought, crimes are committed, and hate grows. It's why a guy who said he wanted to build walls to keep people separated was able to become the most powerful person in the free world.

Me versus them. Us versus them. It happens everywhere. Even in punk rock. Though I personally experienced a lot of openness and acceptance when I first got into punk, it wasn't lost on me that many of us were closed off to other people—like jocks or hippies.

One of my best friends is a *huge* hippie. Like, a 100% fingerpainting, sandal-wearing, Frisbee-throwing hippie. If you looked at the two of us side by side, you'd think we had nothing at all in common. Yet we've been close since the ninth grade. I was somewhat closed off to hippie types back then. I thank my dear friend for opening my eyes, showing me early on that I could find common ground and be great friends with someone so different.

Hippies, punks, jocks, cowboys, whatever-the-fucks—we're all the same. We might live entirely different lives, but we're not as separate as we might think. Deep down we are brothers and sisters, and our differences are great, in both senses of the word. If all the billions of us were the same, it'd be straight-up fucking boring to be human.

And while our differences do indeed make life beautiful, so does our sameness.

Enter "nonduality." It's a difficult concept to grasp. I struggle with it myself. But I have also seen and felt its truth, and it's had a huge impact on me. In one way, the basic idea is this: *we are not separate, we are all connected.* And that means everyone and everything.

Depending on the philosophy or religion, that can be interpreted differently, but it's similar at the core. In yoga and Hinduism there is *Atman*, or Self, and *Brahman*, or God/the "collective universal force." (If hearing about "Atman & Brahman" makes you think of superheroes, that's okay: I think that all the time too. The thought usually comes with a soundtrack too: *Na na na na na na na na AT-man!*) Some paths of yoga hold that Atman and Brahman are actually one in the same and that we are all expressions of Brahman.

Buddhism addresses nondualism by talking about

"form and emptiness" and how the two are really the same thing. Again all is connected, yet separate. The Buddhist teachings tell us that all this is really something to be experienced and not so much talked about, but let me try anyway: When we really quiet our mind or ego, we see for ourselves, in time, that our self doesn't really exist—at least, not in the way we always thought it did. We begin to find that all of the lines we draw between ourselves and others aren't real. Through practice, we begin to catch glimpses of the connectivity that we're part of and see how hurting others ultimately just hurts ourselves. Let's take a look at an example.

Earlier we touched on how everything that has ever happened had to happen for us to be here now. This also means that every person who has ever crossed our path *had* to do so, in the exact way they did, for us to be here now.

That includes the assholes. In fact, they often offer us more than others, in terms of life lessons and opportunities for growth. Like growing? Thank a jerk! (Just remember that as far as that jerk is concerned, he's not a jerk. You might be the jerk. You never know.)

The point here is to make room for everyone, and that includes all their differences and their samenesses too. When we're too concerned with drama and hatred, or just being annoyed, we get pulled further and further away from our perfect day. Don't be so busy living in your head that you miss the beauty in front of you, whether it comes in the form of a moment in nature or a harsh lesson from an asshole. Just accept it, and when it's time to move on, move on.

I'm not sure if I believe in Atman and Brahman or not,

but I do know that the less I live like there's some major difference between myself and others and the more I help others, the more I feel at peace.

You'll recall that some forms of Buddhism talk about the idea of the bodhisattva, someone who seeks enlightenment not only for themselves but for all beings. The bodhisattva even vows to pass up enlightenment until all other beings are enlightened first. This is because the bodhisattva understands that until all beings are free, no one can really be free.

I like to think that we each have a bit of a bodhisattva in us, a part of us that wants to help and accept others. This part knows that because of our interconnectedness, helping and accepting others are really the best things we can do to help ourselves. When we celebrate and appreciate our differences and our sameness, we can reconnect, and suddenly we're back into our perfect day.

Of course, being a full-blown bodhisattva is easier said than done. Just *not being an asshole* takes practice. So let's practice it now.

■ ■ ■

Practice: Metta II

We're going to modify and build on the practice from the last chapter, so this one is also related to the concept of metta, or loving-kindness meditation. This practice is quite condensed, so if a full metta practice is something you want to explore, do. There are plenty of resources out there. (I've included a list of recommended reading at the end of this book. Check that shit out.) For now, simpler is good. Let's go!

1. First, sit comfortably—in a chair, on your knees, on your butt, whatever.

2. Rest your hands anywhere that's comfortable—at the heart center, on your knees, on your butt, whatever. It might help to close your eyes, but if that's uncomfortable or distracting, leave them half-open.

3. Breathe for a few moments to settle down. As your mind begins to calm down, your heart softens along with it.

4. From that place of softness (or *softer*-ness) bring to mind a picture of yourself—as you are today, as a child, as a future version of yourself, whatever. Ideally, this is a version of yourself for which it's easy to feel kindness and compassion.

5. As you hold this image of yourself in your mind's eye, begin to send it/you loving-kindness. Breathing in, say to yourself quietly, *May I be well.* Sit with that for a few breaths. Silently note what it feels like to send yourself that wish. Repeat it: *May I be well.* Sit again with it for a few breaths. Repeat it again: *May I be well.* One more time: *May I be well.*

6. Let go of the image of yourself. Return awareness to your breathing.

7. Begin to bring someone else to mind. It can be literally anyone: a friend, family member, coworker, someone you don't get along with, someone you have a lot of love for. It just needs to be someone you'd like to think would benefit from some kindness. Hold them in your mind's eye and begin to send them that same compassion. Say,

silently, *May you be well.* Sit and breathe with that for a few moments. What does it feel like to send this wish to that person? Repeat it: *May you be well.* Sit for a few more moments. Do this twice more: *May you be well.*

8. Bring yourself back into the picture. Imagine yourself and also the someone else you just sent metta to. Now begin to add others. Maybe it's one or two people, maybe it's everyone at your school or job. Maybe you imagine a group that includes the entire city, country, or planet. Hold this group in your mind's eye and, recalling the loving-kindness you have cultivated so far, begin to allow it to expand. Breathing in, say silently to yourself, *May we be well.* (Remember that you are just as much a part of the group as everyone else.) Repeat: *May we be well.* What would that feel like, if everyone in this group were truly well, if none of them had to suffer? *May we be well.* Soften. *May we be well.*

9. After several moments sitting here, begin to let that image go. Return to your breath, in and out. Rest here for several moments until you feel you are finished.

tl;dr

May I be well. May you be well. May we be well.

11.

A Juvenile Product of the Working Class

LIKE IT OR NOT, WE ALL HAVE WORK TO DO. There's the work we do to survive and thrive in school or to pay the rent, the work we do around the house, the work we do on ourselves, the work we do for the greater good. One way or another, "work" takes up a lot of our time, so it's worth it for each of us to ask ourselves: *Do I really want to just mindlessly plow through my work, hoping to get through the day? Or do I want to take control of it and let it be a source of connection, something that helps me have a more perfect day?*

I get it: some work sucks. I've had my share of jobs that didn't do anything for me except give me some money to spend on dumb shit I didn't really need. We all have. Here's a pro tip: if the *only* reason you are doing something is for money, run away. Money is not enough. Yeah, you need it for a home and to feed yourself, your family, your pets, or to pay for school. It's also nice to have some "extra" money for stuff like traveling or toys. But maybe none of us needs money as much as we've always thought we do. If you spend your entire life working only for money and then drop dead out of nowhere, what good did that money do?

When we're giving up all our time and experiences in order to get the money that might buy future time and experiences, that's not exactly a smart investment. The work we do today is the most important work of our lives, because today is really all we have. So if what you have to do is really, truly crushing you, it's time to do something about it. As we examined earlier in the book, we can't all just up and leave our classrooms, jobs, or unwanted obligations, but we can take steps in a positive direction. And we can do that today. We can start by bringing mindfulness into our work, tuning in to it instead of zoning out. It doesn't matter if you're washing dishes, flipping burgers, sitting at a desk, or working construction. Mindfulness helps us focus on the task at hand, renew our connection, and get free from fantasies about the past and future. (Although if you're working construction, mindfulness can save your life.) That's the first step. And if it's all you ever do, it is enough.

But you can go further still. As we become more mindful about the present moment, things get clearer, and we can start to get a better sense of where our path lies. If you're pouring yourself into your desk job, truly mindful, you may well rediscover why you got into that line of work to begin with. You might even fall in love with your work. If that's the case, rad! But if not, keep up the mindful connection and note what it is that doesn't sit right with you about what you do; a new way forward might reveal itself.

As little kids, we all imagined futures as firefighters, police officers, writers, musicians, athletes, astronauts, and so forth. We all had such huge dreams and desires, and yet most of us at some point lost connection with all that. We traded in our dreams for comfort, stability, money, the illusion of security. And don't be mistaken; security *is* an illusion. Life doesn't care how much we plan or save. So if we have no security anyway, why not spend today doing something we really care about?

What was your dream when you were a kid? What is your dream now?

I ALWAYS HAD MUSIC IN MY HEART, always wanted to be in a band. Now, not everyone can, or should, be in a band. If you don't like hard work, you really shouldn't start a band. If all you want is to be rich and famous, you *really* shouldn't start a band. I love hard work, and here I am, playing bass in not just a band but one of the best bands I could have ever hoped to join. If I were doing this for the money and not the moment-to-moment experience of being in Teenage Bottlerocket, I'd be sorely disappointed.

I still consider the deaths of my mother and sister to have been huge catalysts for the fearlessness that allowed me to follow my dream. But no one needs to die for you to follow yours. We all have the potential to realize what we want to do and make it happen. Yes, it's maybe not going to be easy, but it'll be so worth it. My punk-rock career has had its share of struggles, some that I wasn't sure the band or myself would make it through. We're still here, though, and I think that's because of the music itself. It drove us to push through whatever life threw at us. If money had been at the core of our intentions, we would have quit years ago.

When you are in connection with your heart, it is easier to appreciate what you get. Sure, maybe we aren't selling out stadiums, but we are always playing shows. Maybe we aren't selling millions of records, but that I get to make records at all blows my mind.

So if you want to play music, make time to play music. If you want to write, write. If you want to cook, do it. Hell, if you want to write insurance policies, then write insurance policies. Whatever your work is, do it mindfully, from a place of heart. Don't worry about how big you might get or how much money you hope to make. Even if your bank account isn't full, your heart will be.

That brings us back again to letting go of results and the old "do your best and fuck the rest" approach. One way or another, if you do your best, you *will* be successful—maybe not in the way you've imagined or planned for, but successful nonetheless. In fact, I'd go so far as to say that if you're doing your best, that is, itself, being successful.

Keep your eyes, heart, and mind open, and see where that takes you. Here's a practice to help you along the way.

■ ■ ■

Practice: A Mindful Moment at Work or School

1. Show up early. This gives you some time to establish a connection with yourself. Rather than rushing to get to school or work and then immediately zoning out, we're going to establish mindfulness from the beginning of our day. So yeah, show up early, on purpose.

2. Find somewhere quiet to sit and breathe for a few moments. We've been working on this basic connection to the breath for a while now, so hopefully you have a

routine. As you connect to your breathing and begin to settle your mind, set an intention:

Today I will work with my whole being.

Breathe that intention in. What would it feel like to do each part of your work fully today?

Repeat.

Today I will work with my whole being.

Do this for a few moments, and then . . .

3. Get to work. If you have a to-do list, try to do each thing one at a time, giving each item your full attention before moving to the next. Try to maintain this mindfulness for the first hour of your day, or your first half day, full day, week—whatever you can handle. Take steps that you can keep up with, and enjoy giving your full self to your work.

tl;dr

Show up to school or work early. Sit quietly. Set the intention: *Today I will work with my whole being.* As often as you can, return to that intention all day long.

12.

Give Freely

SITTING WITH MY DOGS THIS MORNING, I was
hit by an overwhelming sense of gratitude: these two little
dudes love me a lot, and I love them a lot back. That's part
of what makes dogs so special. They give what's in their
hearts without expecting anything in return.

That's the main lesson our cuddly, awesome friends
have to teach us: *Give. Give often. Give freely.* (They clearly
have some intense insight into the value of sniffing one
another's butts too, but let's just stick with the giving
freely part.)

"Give what you want to receive" is a concept found in
virtually all spiritual traditions and societies. It's another
way of saying "what goes around comes around." Want
tacos? Give your tacos away. Want money? Give your money
away. There are different ways of understanding what's
really at play here. Some believe a higher power or force
will reward you for giving freely. Others believe that it's
the giving itself that is the true reward. Some chalk it up
to "karma."

Everyone's heard of karma, but most misunderstand it.
They think it's some sort of cosmic justice, a mystical version of "an eye for an eye." This view of karma assumes two
things: first, that there's some Great Scorekeeper keeping

track of a punishment/reward system; and second, that either the past or future actually exists.

Both assumptions are off. Karma is, simply, cause and effect. It's simple, yes—but not as simple as "do bad stuff, and it'll come around and bite you in the ass."

Let's say that there *is* some higher power keeping score, and there *is* a punishment/reward system: *If you're an asshole, you will be punished! If you're nice, you will be rewarded!* Well, okay, but what about the millionaire criminals who build their empires on the backs of innocents? Or the power-hoarders who do whatever they want with impunity? Are their money, fame, and hot wives rewards from the Great Scorekeeper for all the super-beneficial things these assholes secretly did? I call bullshit.

Now let's consider a hardworking, community-activist single mom who's always worked tirelessly for others and ends up diagnosed with a terminal disease at a too-young age. Did she "deserve" that? Of course not. This Great Scorekeeper must be a real asshole then.

Maybe that's why some people say, "Karma's a bitch." But what I think they're really thinking is, "I know who deserves what, and when. I'm on the right side of karma." We all probably think that to some extent.

But stop for a moment and repeat after me: "I don't know as much as I think I do." (This is something I find myself saying a lot.) Even if there were some scorekeeper, we couldn't know how they operate. And, if you're doing nice things just because you expect some sort of reward, you're kind of a child. It's not really "giving freely" if you expect to be paid off with a cushy eternity hanging out on a cloud surrounded by hotties.

Actual karma has nothing to do with rewards or punishments. And if you ask me, it also has little to do with the past or the future. As we've examined in other chapters, the only moment we can ever access or point to is now. So karma is about our actions in the present moment. Karma is *now*.

The problem with rewards, punishments, the past and future, and all this other stuff is that it distracts and disconnects us from the present moment. We can't live our perfect day if we're off in La-La Land dreaming of unlimited taco bars and salsa fountains. Our connected, perfect day is only encountered in what we're doing now. And so we give freely—because we can, and because it honors the connections we share with others and gives us a sense of joy that we can never feel in disconnection.

Remember the idea of "do your best, and fuck the rest"? As in, letting go of results? That applies here. Giving without attachment to results frees you of a huge burden. It allows you to be present. In Buddhism this is called *dana*, which is a Pali word meaning "giving freely" or "generosity." When we engage in dana, our hearts are open. When there is no dana, there is only Zuul. (That's a *Ghostbusters* joke, from the 1984 original. I give it freely to you.)

Many meditation groups and classes operate on a dana basis; instead of charging money, they accept donations. You give what you want, and only if you are able and inclined. What a beautiful concept.

Since stuff is just stuff and none of it is permanent, the act of giving is ultimately a finer gift than any object could ever be. And your giving never needs to be limited to objects or money. You can give a gift through your actions, your words, your time, or even your thoughts. A simple smile is a gift. Even a positive thought toward a person is a gift. When it comes to giving and connecting with others, you have endless resources at the ready.

Here's a practice to help you try out giving freely.

■ ■ ■

Practice: Something for Everyone

For today, we're going to practice giving something to every person we encounter. This might sound extreme, but hear me out. Knowing that we are all in this together, we must do our best to honor and support each other on our paths. Approaching our day with the intention of giving a gift to everyone we cross paths with can help us change our perspective. (I know what you're thinking: *Really? I have to give something to* EVERYONE? This practice might seem unsustainable at first, but over time it can become second nature to walk through life with this sense of giving.)

1. Wake up. As you prepare for your day, set an intention: *Today I will give a gift to every person I meet.* Through thought, speech, and action, your life today will be a gift to others. Today you will give and expect nothing in return.

2. Sit in your morning meditation (as described in chapter 2). After several minutes of quiet breathing, bring your intention for the day to mind. Say to yourself quietly, *Today I will give a gift to everyone I meet.* Sit with this intention for several moments. Repeat, *Today I will give a gift to everyone I meet.*

   Note how this feels. Does it feel liberating or empowering? Or does it feel constricting or scary? There is no right or wrong answer; simply observe your reaction and continue to breathe. Repeat this again: *Today I will give a gift to everyone I meet.* One more time: *Today I will give a gift to everyone I meet.*

3. Sit and breathe for a few more moments. When you are finished with your meditation, resume your day, carrying this intention with you. Keep the intention of giving freely at the forefront of your day. (Write a note on your hand if you have to.)

4. Now, make your intention a reality. Give each person you meet today a gift. If you see a homeless person, give them some food or change, or the simple gift of looking them in the eye and acknowledging their personhood. When you encounter friends or family, tell them something you love about them. Offer everyone in your day a kindness, even if it's just a simple smile or a silent wish for their well-being. Whatever it is, it's enough.

5. Observe how this practice makes you feel. Maybe it's easier to give to people you care about or to complete strangers. Maybe there are people you encounter today that you have resentments toward. It doesn't matter. Give them a gift anyway. Like I said, it can simply be a wish for their well-being. The person doesn't even need to know you are offering them a gift! No matter who they are, give. You probably won't get anything in return, but that's not the point.

6. Do this all day long. Give something to every single person you encounter. At the end of your day, reflect on how giving freely affected the course of your day.

Note if you feel lighter. How has giving freely affected your perfect day?

tl;dr

Sit on your butt and breathe. Set an intention to give a gift to every person you encounter today. Give a gift to every person you encounter today. Whether it's an actual gift or simply a kind thought, give. Know you won't receive anything in return, and give anyway. Reflect on how giving freely changed your day. How do you feel?

13.

Change

WE ALL KNOW THAT THINGS CHANGE. Change, after all, has been happening all our lives. And yet we often find ourselves resisting or fearing it. But if we know that everything really is always changing, why not embrace that as a source of connection, opening our hearts to life instead of hiding in fear and denial?

One way leads us toward our perfect day. The other keeps us a prisoner. What'll it be?

The truth of impermanence, as Buddhism puts it, is that all things are always changing, and our suffering comes not from the changes themselves but from our resistance to them, in the form of clinging and aversion. *Clinging* just means that we want to hold on to certain things. *Aversion* is just wanting to push other things away. With either one, we're trying to control the uncontrollable, and that shit never works—at least, not for long. Only by making peace with the reality of impermanence can we begin to find peace within ourselves.

Changes, of course, run the gamut. Sometimes they can be welcome, even exciting: a raise at work, a better place to live, an opportunity to do something you've always wanted to do. If you've been shoveling dog shit for a living and then suddenly someone offers you a job playing guitar, change may even seem like a miracle.

On the other hand, if you've been with your partner for a decade and they suddenly run off with someone else, that's the kind of change that can be really fucking unwelcome, even terrifying.

Most change falls somewhere in the middle. When my band does a new record, for example, some fans might complain that it's too much like our other records; other fans might complain that we took a risk and did a slow song with strings for a change of pace. Whatever some might want and some might not, change (or lack of it) *is* going to bum people out.

Change is relentless: it comes in an infinite number of forms, and it happens every second of every day. Some changes are subtle: a new pair of shoes, a shift in the direction of the wind, the turning of food into farts. Other changes are less subtle: a new job, a new family member, residence in a new country, divorce, death. No matter how subtle or direct change is, it's all around us, all the time. Right here, right now? *Change.* And once this moment is over, things will be different forever.

So if all things, even *this moment*, are impermanent, how do we deal with it? Well, as my old friend Tony Sly (the late, great singer of No Use for a Name) used to say: we've got options. When he was speaking of options, Tony usually meant what kind of food we could eat or what kind of trouble we could get into that evening; still the sentiment remains the same. We've got options—two, to be exact:

1. We can try to avoid change, forcing ourselves into disconnect and ultimately suffering.

2. We can accept change with an open heart, enjoying the feeling of freedom that comes from flowing with it.

When I was a teenager, I hated high school but loved my friends. One part of me longed to be out on my own as an adult, able to do whatever the fuck I wanted. Another part wanted to hang out with my friends listening to NOFX and building sketchy ramps for our bikes/skateboards forever. I couldn't wait for things to change, and at the same time I wanted some things to stay the same indefinitely. I know you know what I mean.

Now, in my thirties, I can see a few things I couldn't before about those days. I can see that in my rush to be free from the hallways of Laramie High School and out on my own schedule, I missed out on a lot. My head was in the clouds a lot of times, and it caused a fair amount of disconnect.

I can also see that my clinging to my friends caused a lot of suffering—for them and for me. Some grew up and moved away, some I still see today, others I haven't talked to in years. Too many have since lost their lives. There's been lots of change—but back then I had this idea my friends would always be there, so when that didn't prove true, it was hard to deal with. I even lashed out at certain people. It's taken many years to patch up some of those relationships, and some, of course, are beyond repair now.

Around that same time in my life I could see my mother changing—a lot. Cancer can sometimes look like one of the least subtle changes someone might deal with. She was determined to fight it, to be there for her family and outlive her disease. Here she was, the dearest person in my life, becoming even stronger than even she ever knew she could be. She fought that cancer with all of her might, and she beat it the first time through.

The second diagnosis, though? That was a different story, and it would end up being the biggest lesson in impermanence of my life. When it seemed treatments were ineffective, my mother decided to stop fighting and opened her heart instead. She accepted that all this change was beyond her control and her time on Earth was limited. Instead of resisting and fighting, she made a conscious decision to flow with the cancer. She lived the remainder of her days with a fullness of heart that still inspires me all these years later.

I struggled adapting to all the changes her cancer brought. Having a sick mother, and then a deceased mother, was not easy to accept. I spent many years resisting, fighting, running away. There was lots of drug abuse, alcohol abuse, overeating, overspending—overconsuming just about anything to try to escape my feelings. (I should note here that I don't believe there is anything necessarily wrong with using any of those things, even drugs, if it's a source of connection. The problem comes from abuse and disconnect. We'll come back to that later.) The point is I was running, and it was causing me a lot of suffering.

It wasn't until many years later when I began to study impermanence and work with it in my own practice that I began to find peace with her passing. Now I can see that all those changes I was living through were laying out the foundation for the rest of my life.

You see, change isn't only inevitable; it's actually a good thing. I understand that might be a challenging idea to absorb, especially when we're talking about change as profound as the death of a loved one. But, really, without the changes I experienced, I would not—could not—be the Miguel I am today. In watching my mother make peace with giving up her own life, I learned how to live my own life more fully.

That was her gift to me, and it's my hope that I can pass some of what I've learned from it to you, so that you too can be more openhearted and ready for whatever change may come your way. And make no mistake—it's coming. So let's practice.

■   ■   ■

Practice: The Five Remembrances

This is a traditional Buddhist practice on impermanence. Now—as with any practice in this book—you don't need to be a Buddhist or subscribe to any particular set of beliefs to benefit from it. This is simply a contemplation practice, to help you reflect on and make peace with the ever-changing nature of life.

This can be a difficult practice, so if at any point one of the five remembrances seems too heavy, take a break. Maybe only contemplate the first or second remembrance to start, and work your way up to all five. As always, take what works for you, and bail on the rest!

Since most of our practices have been based around a seated meditation posture, you know the routine: find a quiet place, sit comfortably, and take some time to breathe.

1. When you've reached a relatively quiet space in your mind, say to yourself: *I am of the nature to grow old.* Whether or not you want that to be true, it is. We all will get old, unless we die first. (But let's not get ahead of ourselves. We'll deal with death in the third remembrance.) Note how saying "I am of the nature to grow old" to yourself feels. Does it make you uncomfortable? That's okay. Simply sit with whatever arises for a few moments. Then let go of the first remembrance, and make room for the second.

2. *I am of the nature to get sick.* Saying this to yourself silently, note what arises. I don't wanna get sick. You don't wanna get sick either. But it's going to happen, and that's okay, just part of being human. *I am of the nature to get sick.* Sit here for a few more moments, then clear space for the third remembrance.

3. *I am of the nature to die.* Things are getting a bit heavier, so again, if this is too much right now, save it for another day. But if and when you can comfortably work with this step, say to yourself: *I am of the nature to die.* Note what this brings up. Allow any thoughts or emotions to exist. It's natural to feel a resistance here, but it's also possible to find acceptance.

4. Now it's time for the fourth and arguably the heaviest of the five remembrances. Only do this work if it feels safe. Don't be afraid of discomfort, but remember the goal here is to work on openness and acceptance, not to leave yourself traumatized. Here we go: *All that is dear to me and everyone I love are of the nature of change; I will be separated from them.* No matter how hard we

cling to our loved ones, we must say goodbye at some point. Perhaps we aren't completely separated in the long run—I won't get into my theories on what happens after death here—but in this lifetime, we will be separated from our loved ones (and our loved things) at one point or another. Note how saying this makes you feel. *All that is dear to me and everyone I love are of the nature of change; I will be separated from them.* Sit with this for a few moments, then let go.

5. The last remembrance: *My actions are my only belongings; I cannot escape their consequences.*

This remembrance is about karma and how actions define our lives. We might think we "own" a car or a record collection or whatever, but those things, as we know them, are only temporary in and of themselves and don't really belong to us. Our actions, however, we can claim full ownership of. We're the "authors" of them. The consequences of our actions will affect us, whether we want them to or not. How does sitting with this truth feel?

tl;dr

I am of the nature to grow old. I am of the nature to get sick. I am of the nature to die.

All that is dear to me and everyone I love are of the nature of change; I will be separated from them. My actions are my only belongings; I cannot escape their consequences.

14.

Opportunity

ALL DAY LONG, life is offering us choices to make, paths to take. It can be difficult to recognize these opportunities, but they're there, all around us. The more connected we become, the more we perceive these opportunities, and what we choose to do about them can shape our lives. Opportunities, by their very nature, come down to two basic choices: take it or don't. So how do you know what the right choices are for you?

Look to your gut.

My gut, at the moment, is full of pizza. But that's not what I mean. I mean your intuition. We're all born with intuition, but few of us really trust and make use of it. That's too bad, because our intuition is looking out for us, trying to lead us down exciting new paths. Our intuition wants us to live fully—for ourselves, and for the world around us. Our intuition is the fucking coolest.

For me, the difference between just cruising through life unconnected and really, truly living usually comes down to tuning in and fearlessly following my intuition about opportunities. Remember, fear keeps us in disconnect. You can't be afraid to truly live if you want to truly live.

I HAVEN'T SAID MUCH about Teenage Bottlerocket yet, mainly because this book is really about so many other things. But I can't talk about opportunity without talking about TBR. It's given me so many huge opportunities, and—thanks to my intuition—I was able to let go of fear and take them.

I remember the first time I went on tour; I was just a merch guy and van driver at the time. We were out on the road and about six hours away from Laramie, and I was suddenly filled with panic. What if there were an emergency back home? I wouldn't be able to be there right away and might not even know about it for days. I was scared absolutely shitless. But then my intuition stepped in and told me to disregard my fear and keep on driving.

Thank holy fuck that I did. I've now spent over a decade with the band, traveling all over the world, playing shows ranging from two people in Kansas to twenty thousand in Copenhagen. Together we've been all over North America and Europe more times than I can count. We've even been to Russia, Japan, Australia, and Brazil.

Yes, at times it's been difficult, but all in all my life has a new layer of connectedness that I hadn't known before. I'm so grateful for the band and the opportunities it gives me.

Living without fear, recognizing opportunities, knowing when to make a move and when to back off—that's all a huge part of being in a band. But then, it's a huge part of any life, on any path. My dear friend Brandon Carlisle knew this. He knew that following his dreams wouldn't always be easy, but that the alternative was far worse.

When Brandon and his twin brother, Ray, started Teenage Bottlerocket in 2001, they had a pretty clear idea of what they wanted the band to be. They came up with their name and their logo, and began writing songs and playing shows. From the get-go, they took opportunities when they were presented and created opportunities where there were seemingly none.

Brandon, in particular, was a real mix of head and heart, following his instinct and his dreams. It wasn't always clear to the rest of us which tours or offers we should embark on, but Brandon always knew. So much of the band's success, I believe, was due to this ability to see a chance for growth and take it.

And that ability wasn't limited to just the band. Brandon was always working on something: building ramps, going fishing, learning how to smoke meat. Every time he saw an opportunity for happiness or fun, Brandon took it. And his intuition was so refined, he always seemed to know when to reach out to people. You'll hear countless stories from friends about Brandon calling out of the blue with perfect timing, right when they most needed a dose of his friendship. You had to love him.

In October of 2015, Teenage Bottlerocket was in Gainesville, Florida, playing "The Fest"—a yearly punk-rock festival down there, one of the greatest in the world. We were having the best time of our lives. I had been taking it easy, not partying much or really even being particularly social.

For some reason, my gut told me to make extra time with Brandon in Gainesville. So my girlfriend (now wife) Lily and I went out with Brandon and his girlfriend after TBR played. We had the best night ever, really talking about life, the band and how far we'd come, and how blessed we were.

A few short days later Brandon fell into a coma. A few days after that, he was dead. The official cause of death was pancreatitis. How he could have that going on and not have known it will remain a mystery forever.

What we know for sure is that Brandon lived an amazing life, never afraid to follow his gut and seize opportunities. In many ways, it's thanks to his fearlessness that my own life has been what it has. But the biggest gift he gave us, even more than the music, was the example he set for everyone. He taught us to live from the heart, to take opportunities, and that we have to do it today, because it could all be over tomorrow. Rest in peace, my dear friend.

May we all live like Brandon. May we all see the opportunities we are given, use our intuition, and live the fullest lives possible.

■ ■ ■

Practice: Fire Escapes

This practice is based on a meditation called *trataka*, or yogic gaze. The idea is to work on single-pointed awareness, so we can release ourselves from the grip of distraction and develop our intuition. If you study yogic gaze you might hear a lot of talk about "third eyes," chakras, and that sort of thing. Personally, I enjoy investigating these ideas, but don't believe you have to to gain some benefit from yogic gazing. All you'll need is your breath and a candle. Here we go!

1. Find a quiet place, free from distractions. As with most of the other practices in this book you will benefit

greatly from leaving devices behind, putting the dogs outside, and finding a quiet, clean room.

2. Find a candle. Any candle will do, though an unscented candle will probably be less distracting than *Lavender Ocean Breeze* or *Tropical Toucan Fart* or whatever.

3. Find your comfortable seat, on a cushion, a bench, or the floor, the same as any other sitting meditations we've done so far. You want to be a few feet away from the candle.

4. Set the candle on a coffee table or shelf, so that it's around eye level.

5. Light that candle up!

6. Take a few mindful breaths. Keep breathing.

7. Focus your gaze on the candle; specifically, the flame. As best you can, release your mind's need to grip on any particular thoughts. Drop distractions and just look at the flame. If the mind wanders, gently note the wandering, and softly return awareness to the flame.

8. After a while your eyes might begin to get a little sensitive. When they do, close them. As you close your eyes, you may notice a silhouette, or afterimage, of the flame. Bring your awareness there. Focus on this afterimage until it fades away.

9. Repeat as many times as feels appropriate.

So what are we doing here? We're really just giving the mind something to focus on, and at the same time training ourselves to be able to let go of distractions. Some say that focusing on the afterimage of the flame helps develop the third eye, which helps us see things as they really are. I say it just helps our brain shut up a little, so our heart can speak up.

tl;dr

1. Quiet room—go find one.

2. Candle—find one of those too.

3. Sit and breathe.

4. Set the candle at eye level.

5. Light that shit.

6. More sitting and breathing.

7. Focus your gaze on the flame.

8. Close your eyes, focus your gaze on any afterimage of the flame that remains.

9. Repeat.

15.

Bullshit

So: where're we at?

Let's take stock. If you've been taking to heart the ideas and practices we've been talking about so far, then:

- You're sitting in meditation, maybe more days than not, and bringing the mindfulness you're cultivating while sitting into the rest of your life, trying to keep an open heart and a calm mind.

- You're beginning to practice giving freely, expecting nothing in return.

- You have a basic understanding of karma, which makes it so you know that acting from a place of kindness can help you to realize a perfect day.

If all that's going on, things might be going pretty well for you. And yet, as you bring awareness and connection into your daily life, you might begin to notice: *there's still a lot of bullshit to deal with!* You've been honestly trying to practice compassionate living for a while now, so when does all the bullshit—all the problems in your mind and all around you—just *stop*?

It doesn't.

I wish I could tell you that if you sit on your ass, breathing and staring at a wall long enough, you will suddenly find yourself in a bullshit-less existence, where everything is always awesome and nothing is ever terrible. I wish I could tell you that practicing mindfulness would mean you never had to feel pain again and that everything would always go your way. I wish I could tell you the bullshit ends, but . . .

The bullshit doesn't end. Our lives will always have struggle and hardships. It's just part of the human experience. So if we can't escape these hardships, what can we do? Should we just give up on trying to have our so-called perfect day?

No! No matter what life presents us, we always have a choice in how we react to it. Even in the face of the biggest bullshit you've ever encountered, you still have choices: Do you let yourself be a victim? Do you fall into a trap? Or do you see and take an opportunity?

You might think this "perfect day" we keep talking about would be one without any struggles or hardships. But that's not reality. Hardships are always part of life, and what's more, they can help set you free. We *need* them so we can really appreciate life. If everything were always peaches and cream—does anyone actually eat "peaches and cream"?—we'd never really understand what a gift it is to be alive. So we have to accept bullshit as a part of our path.

In Buddhism, there is a huge distinction between pain and suffering. Pain is an inevitable part of being a person. Someone smacks you with a huge rubber paddle? *Pain.* Got your foot run over by a car? *Pain.* Your mom dies of cancer when you're sixteen years old? *Pain.* You cannot escape pain. (Ooh, now I sound like Pinhead from *Hellraiser.*)

Suffering, on the other hand, is unnecessary and, with practice, can be let go of. Remember: suffering is not the pain itself but how we react to it. There will always be times when we will feel pain, but our *suffering* comes from how we relate to it.

Let's refer back to what we've learned about breathing. Our breath, our constant companion, can be a great teacher. When we feel pain, we often try to run away and avoid feeling it. This is like refusing to breathe in. Other times, we get addicted to, or at least comfortable with, our pain and can't see that we're stuck. This could be seen as like refusing to breathe out. In or out, if we don't breathe, we're going to fucking die. This is the lesson of clinging and aversion. We don't suffer because of the pain we feel—we suffer because we can't accept things as they are.

I've related in previous chapters how the deaths of friends and loved ones have affected me. My initial reaction to try to avoid the pain and to try to hold on to people I couldn't hold on to did nothing but cause suffering. This is classic clinging and aversion: something we all do, and something we can all work to stop. And when we do finally confront our pain, we can see that we're stronger than we thought we were. We can even see that our experience of pain is a crucial part of our path.

I'VE KNOWN MANY PEOPLE who would consider themselves drug addicts or alcoholics. Some of them were my closest friends, and many of them have died. Others are still doing battle with themselves and their addictions. Others have come out the other side, stronger than ever.

Now, I'm hesitant to write too much about drugs or substance abuse, because I don't think that using, in and of itself, is automatically wrong. Like any other thing in life, it can be a source of experience—or a source of disconnect. The problem doesn't come from the substances alone, but rather how we relate to them.

Full disclosure? I have done a lot of drugs in my life, drank a lot of alcohol, and at one time was a pack-a-day smoker. I've struggled with overeating, overspending, oversexing—just about anything one could *over*do. Nowadays, I try not to abuse these things. I still eat, of course. I still have sex. I'll still smoke a cigarette here and there. And while my drug days are behind me, my drinking days are not—though I relate to alcohol differently than I used to, being mindful not to drink too often. (I'll admit, though, that "too often" seems to be a fluid concept in my story.) My point is that this is *my* life, and these have been *my* struggles. Yours may look similar or nothing like mine. That's as it should be! You and I are different people, and so we'll face and handle different challenges differently.

This seems like a good time to say—whether you're doing all the things we just mentioned or none of them, or somewhere in between—you don't have to give up anything you don't want to. I can't tell you what is right or wrong for you. Only you can know what you need to do. Be honest with yourself and follow your intuition, and you'll see.

Also look around you. If you've ever met someone who's going through recovery, you may have thought they seemed very connected to life—brave, open, and with a higher appreciation of what it means to be a human. They have learned the lessons of their pain and have begun to wake up. They are amazing examples of the strength and potential we all have. So make friends with them and learn from them.

If you have had struggles with drugs or alcohol and have come to a place of abstinence, congratulations and thank you. So many of us go through life never facing our pain, never learning the lessons that would allow us to open our hearts and take real care of ourselves. That shit is not easy! But you are an amazing example of strength and potential.

Whether it be addiction, loss, heartbreak, or any other form of pain, there's no getting around it: we'll have to experience it. But we do have a choice. Will we allow this pain to make us suffer, or will we allow it to open our hearts?

You know what the better choice is. So let's get used to opening our hearts in the face of suffering.

■   ■   ■

Practice: Bare-Bones Tonglen

Tonglen is a Buddhist meditation practice. In tonglen, we make a point of actively engaging with that which we typically find uncomfortable and letting go of what brings us pleasure.

Tonglen can be practiced in many stages; to start, we will focus on the very first steps only.

1. Find a quiet spot to sit and breathe for a while. As with so many of the other practices in this book, we'll use the breath as an anchor to calm our minds and open

our hearts. So take a several moments to just breathe. Once you have come to a place of relative stillness, it's time to begin tonglen.

2. Breathe in. As you inhale, imagine you are breathing in hot, heavy, uncomfortable air. You might visualize this as actual pollution or the sadness or suffering of someone. Pausing for a moment, notice how it feels to intentionally put yourself here, face to face with discomfort.

3. Breathe out. Here we practice giving, letting go of things we might normally hold on to. As you breathe out, imagine the air from your lungs is cool, refreshing, and beneficial, bringing relief to someone who needs it. What does this feel like? There's no wrong or right answer; simply observe.

4. Alternate between the in- and out-breaths for a while. Take in the seemingly "bad" air, breathe out and give away the seemingly good air. Note any discomfort that arises, and let it exist without clinging to it.

5. After a while, return to a normal breath, and allow yourself to unwind if needed. Once you feel balanced again, get up. Try to carry this same willingness to face the bullshit with you throughout the day.

tl;dr

Breathe in the bullshit. Breathe out the good stuff. Face the uncomfortable and give away freely that which you would normally try to keep.

16.

Sorry Song

WE WANT TO CONNECT, and we want to have a more perfect day. But we're distracted from that by what we're carrying. And it's really just needless baggage. I'm talking about the guilt, remorse, and sadness we have, addressed or not, from hurting people over the course of our lives. We've caused harm to others, and that has harmed us too. If we really want to be free, we have to learn to say it: "I'm sorry."

Yeah, yeah, I know: People have wronged you too. You shouldn't have to apologize unless they do first. And they were more wrong than you anyhow. *Blah blah blah.* It's all just ego bullshit. The good thing is, you can just knock it off.

You see, your ego thinks it's superior. It always wants to be right. It's always judging others. It even thinks that *it* is *you.* But remember: You're not your ego. You are more than that.

When we work to calm our minds and open our hearts, we see that we are connected to others—even those we have harmed or who have harmed us. Apologizing is a true realization of those connections, and it helps us let go of our needless baggage and move forward unencumbered—or at least less encumbered.

If you're familiar with twelve-step recovery programs, then you probably know that admitting our wrongs, accepting responsibility, and making amends can transform and heal. I myself have never gone through a recovery program, but I've found that applying some of these same principles to my own life has been incredibly helpful. I know there's a lot of God talk in recovery—which doesn't work for everyone—and that you may not even have a need to stop drinking, using drugs, or whatever. That's not the point here. The point is to allow yourself to be open, so if there is something you can do that can help you be better, you can take advantage of it, using what serves you and leaving the rest.

As for me, I've found five of the twelve steps to be especially relevant in my own life. (I've amended them to leave out some of the language that sometimes trips people up. If you're looking for the full steps, in the original language and context, you'll find them in Bill W.'s *Alcoholics Anonymous,* also known as *The Big Book.*) Note that they're in the past tense, suggesting that they've been successfully ticked off of a list of Things to Do—that is, they're things that actually have been done by people, and so *we* can do them too. Here we go:

- Step 4: We made a searching and fearless moral inventory of ourselves.

- Step 5: We admitted to ourselves, another human, and any higher power the exact nature of our wrongs.

- Step 8: We made a list of all people we had harmed, and became willing to make amends to them all.

- Step 9: We made direct amends to such people wherever possible, except when to do so would injure them or others.

- Step 10: We continued to keep a personal inventory, and when we were wrong, we promptly admitted it.

Some of the other steps involve giving our will over to God, asking for God's support, and so on. If that's helpful to you, cool. But I don't think a huge discussion on God or higher powers is necessary right now, so let's just dissect these steps from a more personal perspective.

Step 4 of making a "fearless moral inventory" of yourself takes guts. It's really fucking hard to sit and take a look at yourself, leaving nothing out—even the shittiest, most harmful things you've done. But making that effort can really help set you free. So see if you can stop and take a look at yourself. Ask yourself when and how and to whom you've caused harm. Be gentle on yourself, though, by keeping in mind that these are *things you've done*, not *who you are*. So you've been super-shitty in the past? Well, so have we all, and now is a new moment. You are basically good, and you can take the lessons of the past to promote goodness in yourself and in others.

Now that you've begun to look at the harm you've caused, you can begin to admit the exact nature of your wrongs to yourself, to someone else, and (if you believe in one) a higher power. That's step 5. Again, a higher power may or may not be part of your worldview. Either way, you can and should admit these things to yourself, because you are the one who has to do this work. And you can and should admit these things to another person, because it helps you be accountable and it's good to be heard. That other person can offer support and show you you're not alone. (I think the same goes for the higher power idea, but again if that's not your jam, no worries—and note that steps 6 and 7, which are all about God, have been left out here.) Just begin to take responsibility.

Step 8 is heavy, but powerful. In step 8 we make an actual, physical list of people we have harmed, whether intentionally or not. I'm not going to lie to you: this can be fucking brutal. If you want to feel bad about yourself, do step 8 without any form of self-compassion. You'll be left with just a list of all the shitty things you've ever done and the unfortunate souls who were affected by them. But really, don't try that; we're here to move forward, and being compassionate toward yourself is part of that. Know that the fact that you've harmed others doesn't make you a bad person. You stumbled, as we all do. Remember your basic goodness, and acknowledge that you are trying to right your wrongs.

This leads us to the second part of step 8: *We became willing to make amends*. This willingness to make amends stems again from the basic goodness we're talking about. It means you are a human being and have every right to a fresh start that everyone else does.

In step 9, we start to make amends to anyone we can, unless doing so would be harmful to them. That part is super-important: what good is apologizing to someone if they can't receive it or to do so would just cause further problems? Sometimes we cannot make amends, and even that is part of the process. In those cases we can still breathe, send thoughts of loving-kindness, and open our hearts. But don't let that be your easy way out. Whenever you can safely make amends, you should do just that.

Step 10 is about keeping our eyes open; this is not a one-and-done practice. We keep on paying attention to that personal inventory, and when we are wrong, we admit it. This is fucking huge. Just because you've cleaned your slate doesn't mean you're in the clear forever. We're humans; fucking up is part of *what we do.* But we can become more mindful of *when* we do fuck up and try to make things right each time.

A few years back, I was inspired to do some work cleaning up some past wrongs, so I could let go and move forward. As part of this, I decided to do heavy work on making amends.

If I were going to die, I needed to right at least some of the wrongs I had caused. And so I made a list.

Old friends, enemies, family members, ex-girlfriends, anyone I could think of that I had harmed—they all made the list. Then, I contacted them, one by one, writing them letters that let them know what was going on in my life and asking for their forgiveness.

Doing this changed my life. Now, there were a few people I couldn't contact, either because I couldn't find them or because I thought I might cause further harm. But I was able to reach and communicate with the majority of the people on my list. I was lucky: nearly every person I contacted was receptive to my attempts at amends. I felt so light and free. And while some people did not accept my apology, that's just part of the deal—we can't control whether or not others will forgive us, but making an honest attempt at amends can *still* free us.

By sidelining my ego and apologizing, I was able to let go of so much baggage. This allowed me to heal and move forward. I believe this practice saved my life. I know it can help you too. Get warmed up with this practice.

■   ■   ■

Practice: Amends

In this practice we're going to work with step 9 from Alcoholics Anonymous. Again, I think this practice is universally helpful, so even if you don't have a substance-abuse problem or believe in a higher power, it's worth a try. Take from it what is valuable to you, and don't worry about the rest.

Making amends can be a very healing process, but it can also stir up a lot of shit. For that reason, we're going to start simple.

1. Think of a time when you've hurt someone but haven't yet apologized for having done so. Maybe you borrowed something from a friend and forgot to return it. Maybe you were the wrong one in an argument and never admitted it. I wouldn't try to start with someone you've really, really hurt. For now, just think of a simple event where you were wrong and you owe someone an apology.

   What comes up when you think of this? Maybe apologizing for something small seems kind of pointless, but I assure you, even the small baggage adds up. It's also possible that this seemingly small thing was more hurtful than you thought it was. If nothing else, apologizing for the small things helps us build to making amends for our bigger wrongdoings.

2. Next, prepare yourself to contact this person. If you can talk to them face to face, that would be ideal, but a phone call or message may well suffice. Use your best judgment on what is appropriate for this situation. Ask yourself, *will attempting to make amends hurt this person further?* If you suspect that the answer is yes, move on to a different person/event and start over. If the answer is no and making amends will be a positive thing, get to it.

3. Talk to the person you have wronged. Admit to them that what you did was wrong, you regret it, and you would like to make things right.

4. Listen to their response. This is a two-way street. If you simply say your bit and neglect the response, then you aren't really apologizing sincerely. So pause, and really hear them out. This increases the likelihood that the conversation will end with both of you feeling better about things. NOTE: *It has to be said that your apology may not be met well, so you should be prepared for that possibility. If your apology is not accepted, at least you can move forward knowing you tried.*

5. If anything needs to be done in addition to your apology, make a plan to do it. If you ate all your bandmate's chips while they were asleep, buy them a new bag. Promise it won't happen again—and *mean* it.

tl;dr

That's it. Own up to your wrongdoings, make things right when and how you can, and then let go. That baggage no longer belongs to you.

17.

Finer Points of Forgiveness

CAN YOU THINK OF A TIME when someone hurt *you?* And I don't mean like they smacked you in the face. More like, intentionally or not, it felt like they pulled your heart out of your chest and ground it out like a cigarette. It fucked you up, making you incredibly sad or angry. Maybe you still are.

You probably had no problem just now recalling feeling like that. It happens to us all. I can think of a ton of times when I have been hurt by others, whether they'd really meant to do it or not. I've been hurt by friends, family members, loved ones; I've even had arguments with my bandmates that I didn't think we'd get past. And you can bet your ass I've held resentment. I've resented others for what I perceived to be "them" fucking with "my" happiness.

But like our other extra baggage, we don't have to carry our sadness, anger, and resentment around with us forever. If we want to be free and live our lives fully, we have to put that shit down.

The truth is no one really has control over anyone's happiness but their own. Stay with me now. In the first chapter I mentioned the book *The Four Agreements* by Don Miguel Ruiz (and Janet Mills). You remember: my friend's mom had given me the book because I was being a little shithead and needed to wake up and knock it off. The basic premise is that we can make four agreements to live a more fulfilling life, and while the whole book really did cause me to look at myself, one part is particularly relevant to our work here and has had the biggest effect on my life. It's Ruiz's second agreement: *Don't take anything personally.*

The idea is that we are all living our own story, so when someone makes the decision to hurt you, it actually has nothing to do with you. Instead, it's a part of *their* story. Even if someone were to literally stab you in the chest, Ruiz would say that's about *them*, not you. When I first read this stuff, my teenaged brain almost exploded. But when I took a moment to really think about it, I realized Ruiz was right. People weren't out to get me. They just wanted to live their lives. Even when they did hurt me, it wasn't *about* me.

The more I understood that it wasn't about me, the more relief I felt. And all this made it easier to let go of resentment and move on with my life.

Resentment is our ego's way to try to protect us from being hurt again. But this so-called protection brings with it a lot of disconnect and is really a delusion anyway since we can't ever completely protect ourselves from pain. Pain is a part of the human experience. But remember that just because we feel pain doesn't mean we need to suffer. Pain is not suffering. Pain is pain, and suffering is a reaction to pain.

When people hurt me, whether intentionally or unintentionally, I have a choice. It's easy to choose to blame others for our own suffering, but what good does that really do? It just keeps us suffering. The only choice that leads to *freedom* is to take responsibility for ourselves. When we realize that others' actions might have nothing to do with us, when we see that some shit is our problem and some shit is not, life proves a lot more manageable.

Forgiving others doesn't mean that the things they did are okay. It doesn't mean that we need to let them hurt us again either. What forgiveness means is that we are letting go of resentment, opening our hearts, and making a decision to move forward. It's not always the easiest thing to do, but like many other practices in this book, consistent effort over an extended time can really make a difference.

Yes, forgiving others can be difficult. After all, we've spent most of our lives in an us-versus-them mentality, and that can be hard to shake. But resentment doesn't serve us or move us forward. Resentment belongs in the Shit That Is Not Our Problem pile.

So, forgive people. It doesn't matter if they hurt you on purpose or by accident. It doesn't even matter if you think they "deserve" forgiveness or not. The only thing that matters here is opening your heart so you can live happily. If you find yourself caught thinking, "they don't deserve my forgiveness," remember: (1) Their actions weren't about you, so you don't have to take it personally. (2) None of us are totally innocent. (Myself included, of course.)

In fact, now it's time to think back to an occasion when it was *you* who hurt someone. It should be something you perhaps feel a lot of remorse for: maybe you smacked them in the face or pulled their heart out and stomped on it. How does it feel to know you've caused such suckage?

It can be very difficult to deal with, I know. Through my thoughts, words, and actions, both intentionally and unintentionally, I have caused harm. I've done a lot of things I'm not proud of. I have hurt others. Forgiving myself has been and continues to be one of the biggest parts of my work. Some days I can do it. Some days I can't quite. Some days I fail so hard it's straight-up harsh. But I keep trying, because the moments where I do make progress are worth it.

One thing we should remember is that even though we've caused harm to others, we are still basically good. Whether it seems like it or not, when we've messed up, we were probably doing the best we could at the moment. So we must also be willing to forgive ourselves and give ourselves the unconditional love we deserve.

Whether it's our own actions or those of others, nothing from the past can be changed. We were doing our best, they were doing their best; we are here because of what's happened before. We are the same in our ability to do good, to cause harm, and to forgive. If we want to live our perfect day, we must learn to forgive others and ourselves. Here's a practice to get us started.

■ ■ ■

Practice: Forgiving

Again, this practice starts with some quiet sitting. So find a place free from distraction, take a comfortable seat, and breathe for a few minutes. Use this as an opportunity to clear your mind As you begin to open your heart to the idea of forgiveness, use this time as an opportunity to try to settle your mind a bit.

Even though we may understand that forgiveness can be very healing, it can be challenging. For this reason, we will take up a meditation that cultivates internal forgiveness before we move into the external world.

Once you have practiced mindful breathing for a few moments and have come to a place of relative stillness of mind, it is time to begin.

1. Begin by bringing to mind someone you feel has caused you harm. Start small. Bring to mind someone who has harmed you but you aren't completely uncomfortable working with in your mind. It will be easier to begin this practice by thinking of someone who cut you off in traffic, for example, rather than someone who really jammed you up in the past. The idea isn't to traumatize yourself by revisiting all of the times you've been hurt, but rather to take small, manageable steps toward liberation.

2. Hold this person in your mind's eye. How does this make you feel? What emotions arise when you imagine this person who has harmed you? Anger? Sadness? Fear? Whatever arises, simply take note. It's okay for these emotions to arise. But it is also okay to let them go. And so we start to open to the idea of forgiving them.

3. Still holding this person in your mind's eye, and in your heart too, say (as if to them): *I forgive you.* How does that feel? Do you feel resistance or relief? Either is natural.

4. Repeat it: *I forgive you. For all of the ways you may have caused me harm, I forgive you.* Being aware that this person may or may not have meant to hurt you,

again offer the words, *I forgive you—for any way you may have caused me harm, intentionally or unintentionally, through action, speech, or thought. I forgive you.* Keep noting whatever arises as you begin to offer this forgiveness free from judgment. If this practice doesn't come naturally, understand that that's okay. We're simply practicing.

5. Keep sitting for a few moments. Then, over time, let go of any images of this person you are working to forgive. Allow any accompanying feelings to gently drift away as well. Simply return to the very easy, nurturing breath. In. Out.

tl;dr

Sit quietly, holding space for someone who has hurt you. Offer them the following: *I forgive you—for any way you may have caused me harm, intentionally or unintentionally, through action, speech, or thought. I forgive you.* Sit with whatever arises.

18.

I Like Food

No, I don't *like* food.

I fucking *love* food. I love cooking it, I love smelling it,
I love eating it, I love *loving* it. (No, not like that . . .) For
real though, food rules. And since no day, perfect or not, is
quite right without it, let's examine our relationship to it.

Growing up with a mixed background, I was exposed to
all sorts of cuisine. My mom made a special point of intro-
ducing her kids to a diverse range of delicious foods. A lot
of it, I loved. (Some, not so much. I remember once family
friends brought over a tub full of brains, which my mom
lovingly cooked for us. *Barf!* I couldn't hang.) Mostly, my
youth was all about awesome food: tacos, dumplings, noo-
dles, desserts. I don't think I really knew how good I had it.

As an adult, I still love food. Of course, on tour we're
often so busy that we end up eating a lot of fast food,
but I take every chance I get to find something local and
awesome: burritos in California, pizza in New York, fried
rice in Philly . . . and sandwiches just about everywhere,
especially St. Louis and Montreal. When I'm home, I'm
slow-cooking green chili, making soup, and working on
meals that often take the better part of a day to prepare.
I've always approached food with a real sense of appreciation. Many an ex-girlfriend has said I make sex-like

noises when I'm enjoying a meal, and there's a running joke in Teenage Bottlerocket about what I'm like when I'm eating. All my life, eating was about intense connection—until it wasn't.

At some point food became less about appreciation and more about excess, shoveling as much stuff in as I could to try to appease what had become an unstoppable appetite. This wasn't a physical appetite; it was coming from deeper down. Some sense of longing that I didn't understand was trying to negate itself with whatever was available: drugs, booze, food. Of course, that didn't work. It never could.

Food, like anything else in life, can be either a source of connection or a source of disconnect. Therein lies the food dilemma.

On one hand, we need it to live. That's part of being human: eat food, make energy to function, poop out the rest, repeat. Without food, we are *done-zo*. Beyond that, food can help us nurture our connection to ourselves and, when we share in it, to others. It can be a source of great joy.

Still, overeating, undereating, bingeing, purging, dieting, eating things that don't agree with us: bad relationships with food come in many forms. And while I've never been anorexic, bulimic, morbidly obese, or starving, I have definitely struggled with my relationship to food. If you deal with any of those more extreme struggles, my heart is with you. I wish you strength on your path. Many of us will never know what you are going through. Most of us will, however, experience some degree of disharmony in our relationship to food. It's hard not to.

Look: I'm not a nutritionist, a doctor, or any other kind of expert on what you should and shouldn't put in your body. I'm not here to tell you what to do. But if, like me, you find yourself struggling, you might also find that a little mindfulness helps you uncover what will work for you.

How? Well, mindfulness is all about paying attention. So pay attention. Pay attention to your feelings, your body, your spirit, your eating habits. Are you enjoying your meal? Is it connecting you to life? Or are you watching TV, texting, and shoveling some garbage into your face all at the same time and not really noticing any of it?

And when you're paying this attention, make sure you listen to your heart, and not what others might think. This is *huge.* My dear friend Emily Brown runs a program called BodyLove, all about intuitive eating and the relationship we have with our food and our bodies. The BodyLove premise is simply to eat to nurture yourself—body and soul. Emily puts a lot of emphasis on *accepting* your body instead of trying to fit into a stereotype of what you should look like.

After all, all bodies are different. Some people are big, some people are small, some have a mole or are missing a limb or . . . well, you get the point. People are different. And it's fucking awesome. Don't base the food you do or don't put into your body on some idea that you're not good enough. You are not only good enough, you are fucking awesome.

So the idea is to put (or not put) things into our bodies based on what will nurture our connection with ourselves. Sometimes it might be a salad. Sometimes it might be pizza—you have to nurture your spirit as well as your body, and I can't lie: sometimes, pizza nurtures my spirit. This isn't about going on some crazy diet and being miserable. It's simply about finding your place on the middle path of food.

So eat a little less garbage. Cook for yourself once in a while, not just because it might be healthier but because cooking can be such a rich source of connection and joy. Other times, go ahead and eat a little garbage, and let someone else do the cooking. Most of all, try to bring a little bit of love into the way you see food. Here's a practice to help you along the way.

■　■　■

Practice: Mindful Eating

Today, rather than rushing through eating, let's try a simple mindful eating practice instead. Find a time of day when you won't need to rush and a quiet place free from distraction. Turn off your phone, TV, stereo—anything that might pull your attention away. We're going to be eating, and nothing else.

1. Grab your favorite snack—a piece of fruit, chocolate, a bowl of cereal, whatever you like.

2. In your comfortable spot, pause for a moment. Take a moment to connect to your breathing and try to clear your mind of clutter.

3. Pick up your snack and take a single bite. Set the rest down. If it helps, allow your eyes to close down as you mindfully chew this one single bite. During this first bite simply notice: *What does this food taste like? What is the texture like? What other thoughts arise as I am chewing?*

4. When you're done with that first bite, pause for a moment, and then take another. If it suits you, allow

your eyes to close. Take a moment for gratitude and enjoy this bite. This food gives you nourishment and joy. Thanks to food we can continue living. After this bite is gone, again pause.

5. Take another bite. Chew slowly, mindfully. Enjoy the act of eating without distraction. Repeat until your snack has been consumed.

6. When you are finished, pause one last time. This moment of nourishment is finished, and now it's time to move forward with your day.

Do this practice every once in a while to remind you to reconnect to your food. Even if it's only once a week, that's something. If you're practicing mindful eating every day, you're ruling. Do as much as you can do comfortably.

tl;dr

Grab some food and eat it, but *slowly*. And mindfully. If you blow it, start aagain. One bite at a time. There you go! Proud of you.

19.

Let's Talk about Feelings

SINCE WE'RE WATCHING WHAT goes *into* our
mouths, maybe we should also be concerned with what
comes *out* of them. I'm talking, of course, about barf.

Just kidding. I'm talking about *speech.* It's the most
important tool we have for interacting with others. Since
our perfect day involves relating to others as well as ourselves, maybe we should think about just what the fuck
we're saying.

So what am *I* saying? It's simple: don't say "fuck." Just
kidding—*fuck* is only a word. Though there *is* a huge difference between saying "Go fuck yourself" and "This cake
is fucking delicious!" And there's also a big difference
between saying "Go fuck yourself" with the intent to harm
someone or the intent for the recipient to laugh. Intention,
my friends: it's fucking huge.

The Buddhists talk about all of this in terms of what
they call "right speech." Let's have a look.

Buddhism's "eightfold path" lays out a road to freedom from suffering (*dukkha*). Of these eights aspects of
the path, the third is right speech, or *samma-vaca.* Right
speech more or less boils down to don't lie, don't be harsh
or divisive with your speech, and avoid gossip. In other

words: take care in what you say and how you say it. Let's look closer.

For starts, there's lying (or, rather, *not* lying). That seems pretty rudimentary. Lying causes problems. Even when we're lying just to try to cover our asses, it'll probably catch up with us and make things worse. So don't lie.

But wait: what if, say, you need to tell a white lie to make sure your boyfriend doesn't find out about the secret birthday party you're throwing him? That's different. There's a difference between keeping a surprise and lying as an act of hurtful deception or violence. The main thing is, don't be an asshole.

Okay—so what if the lie involves protecting someone's feelings? Couldn't telling a truth this person wouldn't want to hear about themselves be considered an act of violence? This gets tricky. Sometimes the truth hurts, but it helps set someone on the right path. Sometimes there are ways to say what you want to say, even if it's difficult, without being harsh. Sometimes it's best to not say anything at all. Every scenario will be different, so just try to do your best. You'll almost always find that saying nothing or telling the truth will cause less harm in the long run.

Next up: don't be harsh with your speech. Some might say that this is telling us things like don't swear. If that's true, well, I've fucking blown it. To me, the point here is not to say things to people with the intention of causing them harm. If you're going to cuss, don't do it to hurt. Try to make sure that what you say is kind, or at least not unkind. *Comprende?*

As for avoiding divisive speech, that just means we shouldn't say things that will cause disagreement or hostility between people. Okay, hold the phone: does that mean that, if our opinion might cause a little disagreement, we're supposed to keep it to ourselves? Not necessarily. There is a time to stand up and say what needs to be said. Before you do, ask yourself: is this that time? Also ask yourself: Is what I want to say the truth? Is it kind? Is it necessary?

If you're spouting off contrarian opinions just to hear yourself talk and cause controversy, that's not right speech. That's being an asshole. But if you're truly standing up for something you believe in and doing so in a kind, productive manner, then your speech isn't necessarily divisive. It might even be seen as unifying. Again: intention matters.

Finally, avoid gossip. This one's hard; gossip is almost addictive. Growing up in a small town as I did, you get pretty used to gossip. Everyone knows everyone's business all of the time. Lies and half-truths spread faster than wildfire, and in the end someone usually gets hurt.

When we gossip, we avoid bringing focus on ourselves and instead create dramas and stories about other people. We hurt others and disconnect ourselves.

When it comes to gossip, I'm just as guilty as anyone else. It's an easy way to kill time in a van. But at the end of the day it doesn't really do any good: at best, it killed the time, which took us out of the present moment. At worst it caused real harm in someone's life, or at least reinforced a negative idea about that person without their even having the chance to defend themselves.

The point of all this is that our speech is powerful, so we should take care with that power. By practicing nonviolence through our speech, we free up a lot of energy, which allows us to open our hearts and live without causing unnecessary drama or bullshit. I know I could use less of both, and I bet you could too. So let's try not to be assholes when we talk—for our own sake and the sake of those around us. Here's a simple practice to try out.

■ ■ ■

Practice: Right Speech

The idea is to stop before you speak and consider three questions before you say what you were going to say. Let's break down each step individually.

Is it the truth? Pausing to consider this question before we speak keeps us from spreading lies, which, as we know, can create a whole world of unnecessary drama and pain. If what you're about to say is a lie, or even a half-truth, you're probably better off stopping right there.

Is it kind? Again, our speech is perhaps the most powerful tool we have for interacting with others. If we are kind with our words, we help spread kindness; if we are assholes, we help spread asshole-ness. So if what you're about to say is mean, whether or not the person it's directed at is there, stop. Just don't.

Is it necessary? This is a tough one. We've discussed how gossiping can seem harmless, but might end up causing a lot of damage. Sometimes we say things just out of boredom or to make small talk. The idea here is that if we are talking just to hear ourselves talk, we're probably better off listening to someone else. Being that humans are social creatures, I don't necessarily think all idle talk is "bad." But let's see if we can practice using our speech to its highest potential.

Your practice is to—as often as possible—pause and consider these three questions before you speak. If you forget to, don't worry. Odds are you've spent most of your life just saying the first thing that comes to mind. Unlearning that habit takes time.

But try. If you find that what you were about to say doesn't pass all three tests, see if you can let it go without verbalizing it.

Then pay attention to how you feel when you've succeeded. Have you better listened to and heard the other person? Do you feel more peaceful for not having said something that you might have regretted on some level?

tl;dr

Is what I'm about to say the truth? Is it kind? Is it necessary?

20.

Music

PLAYING SHOWS, writing songs, recording albums, and most of all, listening to music—it's all a huge part of my life.

I think a lot of this came from my mom. She seemed to always be singing, or playing piano or percussion, or dancing. From an early age, because of her, I saw just how much music could fill people with joy. I wanted a piece of the action.

When I was in second grade, she enrolled me in private guitar lessons. By fifth grade, I was playing saxophone, inspired by Mom's big band records. I kept up with the sax through junior high and high school. I was even offered a full music scholarship at the University of Wyoming. I turned that down, though. I liked the music education I'd had up to that point, but wanted to do things my way.

Rewind a few years to sixth grade. Kids a couple of grades older than I was had gotten into punk rock and skateboards. I'd known about Green Day because, you know, *the radio*, but these kids seemed to be in on a really good secret. One guy had a T-shirt that was a play on the Trix cereal box, but it instead of *Trix*, it said *NOFX*. I had no idea what that meant, but I knew it was rad.

When I finally heard NOFX, I was hooked. I started digging deeper, checking out as many punk-rock bands as I could. Descendents, Ramones, Rudimentary Peni—these bands made me want to play music, loud. Saxophone? Acoustic guitar? I wanted to go *electric*. So I saved up whatever money I could, begged my friends for donations, and bought my first electric guitar: some piece of shit Kramer that still sits broken in my basement. I was thirteen.

I started a band. We sucked—bad. It didn't matter, though: we were having the best time ever. We were coming alive, connected to something.

Of course, we broke up. So I did the only thing you can do in that situation: start another band. All I wanted to do was play music and travel.

Eventually I found myself going on tour selling T-shirts for a band called Teenage Bottlerocket. Then one tour, the old guitarist for TBR had to pull out at the last minute. I had spent so much time with the other guys that I was the natural choice as a replacement. I couldn't believe it: I had just been promoted to a full-time member of my favorite band! They asked if I wanted to play guitar or bass. I said bass, because honestly I thought it'd be easier to learn all the songs in time. Now I'm a bass player.

Now, having spent more than the last decade making records, going all over the world, and playing shows of all sizes with my best friends, I feel so blessed. TBR has gotten to do everything we ever wanted with our music. We've put records out on our favorite labels, toured with our favorite bands, seen so many countries, and all while doing something we love. And music has loved us back, giving our lives shape.

Maybe you haven't dedicated your life to sitting in a van

with your friends and waiting to play shows (or maybe you have!), but I'm willing to bet music has been a companion in your life as well. Rock-and-roll, country, hip-hop, jazz, pop, punk, salsa, klezmer—there's music out there for everybody, except maybe my dad. I don't think he listens to music.

Why do the rest of us love music so much? Because it *really* connects us. When we're really listening, with our whole beings, we can let go of distractions and be fully, 100% connected to the present moment. You know that feeling of being lost in a song? When that happens, you're not lost—you are connected to the music as it unfolds here and now. That's the kind of connection I've been talking about this entire book: the beauty that comes from being fully present with whatever the moment brings. Music can bring us there faster than a lot of things.

And it doesn't have to be a song on the radio. It can be hitting a couple of pencils on a table or a bucket. It can be the song of a bird outside your window at five in the morning.

In bhakti yoga, the yoga of devotion, music is often used specifically as a tool for connection. Part of this connection and devotion is expressed and realized through *kirtan*, a musical form of chanting from the heart. Through kirtan, we leave ego aside and connect to something bigger. For some, that "something bigger" is God; for some, it's nature or the universe. Again, you don't have to see things the same way. Music can connect you to whatever you need connection to, with or without a higher power involved. Take what serves you, and leave the rest. (Some might argue that music in and of itself is a higher power—and I'd be inclined to agree with them.)

Back in the day, kirtan would be about the last thing on

earth I'd ever listen to or participate in. After a couple of experiences with it, though, I've found it to be a pure form of connection, very similar to the connection I feel when playing a show or listening to my favorite Ramones tracks.

Whatever you're into listening to, just remember that music can be a very powerful tool of connection, if you let it. I'm not sure I can imagine a perfect day without it.

So, the next time you need to take a break from the rest of life and find yourself connected to your heart again, give music a try. But don't just throw something on in the background. Listen mindfully. This practice shows you how.

■ ■ ■

Practice: Mindful Listening

Let's spend some time connecting to our deeper selves by mindfully listening to music. Instead of just throwing music on as background noise and doing a hundred other things, let's really listen.

Find a space without distraction near your stereo. If you have a record collection, bust out the vinyl. If you don't, don't worry about it. I'm not a vinyl purist like many of my friends, though I agree it might help in this particular practice. It's totally not necessary though. Grab your favorite record, or CD, tape, mp3, whatever.

Headphones might help for this practice, but again they are not completely necessary. The important thing is to set yourself up to just listen to music and do nothing else. Turn your phone off for a minute. Put away any other distractions. It's time.

1. Set the needle on the record, or push play on your device. Then sit. If it's more comfortable, close your eyes.

2. Listen to the song. Really listen. If your mind is full of clutter, breathe through it and try to gently return your awareness to the song. What does this song do for you? How does it make you feel? Maybe you have specific memories of a certain time and place in your life associated with this song. Whatever it is, try not to get lost in your thoughts about it, but rather just let yourself *feel* whatever the song makes you feel.

3. Once the song is over, hit pause, or pull the needle off the record. Take a moment of silence to absorb the experience before moving on with your day. If you feel so inclined, do this practice again with another song, or (*gasp!*) listen to an entire record from front to back. That's it. Just listen to music. See what happens.

tl;dr

Sit down and listen to a song. Really *listen* to it, so there's nothing but the song—no phone, no breaking news alerts. Just you and the music.

21.

Yoga for Everybody

I THINK A LOT OF PEOPLE COME TO YOGA looking for exercise or something physical but end up getting something a lot deeper than they expected. It was the opposite for me. I had been sitting in meditation for years, and friends liked to tell me that since I liked meditation, I would love yoga.

Right away, I thought, *fuck that.*

Part of what had drawn me to Buddhist meditation practice was the idea of seeing for yourself. I would sit, work to quiet my mind—some days, more successfully than others, perhaps—and I could see, for myself, a very real transformation in my quality of life. What I couldn't see was how trying to tie myself into a knot might also benefit me. It seemed to me to be just a fitness trend. So I wrote yoga off.

Then a woman I was seeing convinced me to try it for a month. In what seems like a blink of an eye, that month turned into years. In terms of connection, yoga has become my second punk rock. I was hooked.

In my very first yoga class, I immediately saw parallels to sitting meditation practice. Moving through yoga, I was able to connect to my breath and to myself, just like in sitting.

I started going to as many classes as I could, practicing on my own, reading all about yoga. Now, I'm a certified teacher and have taken over Blossom Yoga, the studio I'd been teaching at, and started a group called Yoga for Punks. I owe yoga a lot. I even met my wife because we were both yoga teachers (and bassists). So I'm here to set the record straight: yoga is not just a physical practice. And it sure as hell isn't just a fashionable trend. Let's take a look.

HOW OLD IS YOGA? Super-old. Older than that guy at the Loaf & Jug who buys Lotto tickets and pays in pennies. Some say it might be five thousand years old; some say even older. But that doesn't really matter. What matters is what yoga has to offer, and that's a lot.

The *Yoga Sutras* of Patanjali are considered one of the most important texts in "modern" yoga—even though they're thought to have been written around 200–400 BC. (Holy mothballs, Batman! That's old!) In those texts Patanjali, an old yoga dude, brought together teachings from both yoga and Hinduism in what he believed to be a comprehensive set of guidelines for those seeking union (or yoga). Again: if you're religion-phobic, don't let words like *yoga* or *Hinduism* scare you off; this doesn't need to have anything to do with religion if you don't want it to.

The guidelines are broken down into the eight-limbed path to yoga. That's right, eight limbs—like an octopus. And only one of these "limbs" is related to physical practice! And none of them is about trendy Lycra pants! But *all* of the limbs are about connection.

First up, we have the *yamas*, or restraints. We've talked a little about these already, but here's the scoop.

The yamas have to do with how we deal with others. It's basically a list of don'ts—pretty obvious, universal stuff: don't be violent, don't lie, don't steal, don't be excessive or possessive. We've seen in other chapters how the way we treat others can affect us; the yamas are all about that.

Next come the *niyamas*, or observances. These have to do with how we deal with ourselves. They are purity (of body, words, and thoughts), contentment, self-discipline, self-study, and surrender. We can't really connect to the world around us in a meaningful way unless we start with ourselves. In this way, I think the yamas and niyamas share a lot with the eightfold path of Buddhism, as well as the fundamental values of most religions. (For an in-depth look at these first two limbs, check out *The Yamas and Niyamas* by Deborah Adele.)

The third limb is to practice asana, or posture. This is what most people think of when they think of yoga. You take your body and put it in different poses. Sometimes you flow between poses; other times you hold a posture for an extended period of time. There are different ways to use your body for connection, and asana aims to do just that. So there are many types of asana practice. I teach hatha, vinyasa, yin, and restorative yoga. (Try out classes at different studios to find the form that best speaks to you!)

Next up we have *pranayama*, or breath control. In yoga, we are given different breathing techniques that can help us alter our mood, consciousness, and connection level. As we've seen earlier in this book, breath is incredibly powerful: If we don't breathe, we die. And if we do it mindfully, we deepen our connection. To me, the last five limbs, starting with pranayama, relate very strongly to meditation practice. Stay with me.

Once we have worked with our breath, we can move on to the fifth limb, *pratyahara*, or sense withdrawal. By bringing our awareness away from outer stimulation and into ourselves, we cultivate a stronger connection with ourselves. If you're not distracted by those bright colors over here, that loud noise over there, or where that weird smell is coming from, it might be easier to focus on your internal landscape. Shifting our attention in this way sets us up for the next limb.

The sixth limb is *dharana*, or focus. You've probably seen people meditate by staring at something like a candle or water. The idea is that, with work, we can shift our awareness to one thing at a time. That's the exact opposite of the dominant mindset in current society, where we find ourselves checking email, listening to music, brushing our teeth, and taking a dump all at the same time. (I'm exaggerating. *You* don't do that, do you?) The point is, we often lack focus, and working on that can strengthen our connection to the present moment.

Dhyana, or meditation, is the seventh limb. As I said, lots of us start with yoga for physical reasons but end up being drawn to its meditative aspects, which maybe we've never really had experience with before. Then, when we try it, we see that the practice of sitting, breathing, and drawing inward strengthens our connection to both our inner and outer landscapes. Meditation is a huge part of my practice. I'd recommend just about everyone try to do at least five to ten minutes of it a day.

Last, there's the eighth limb, *samadhi*. This is a tough one to describe, and maybe even a controversial one as well. Samadhi is often called oneness, bliss, or enlightenment. Many people see it as the ultimate connection between us and God. (By this point in the book you're hopefully somewhat comfortable taking or leaving any God talk. Same with enlightenment.) I like to think of samadhi as pure connection—whether to ourselves, the world around us, or something higher.

OKAY. So there are your eight limbs of yoga. Now what?

Well, it's less about knowing all the terminology and more about putting these ideas into practice in real life. For me, yoga is another set of tools I can use in my quest for happiness. If I want to reconnect over and over and live a perfect day, why not have all the tools I can? With yoga, you get eight in one!

It might seem like a lot to take in, and it is. So just take what speaks to you now. I suggest trying some yoga classes, maybe practicing asana once in a while, but if that's not for you, fine. You may not be able to do all of these steps every day or every week, but you can start to incorporate one here and there. Here's a simple practice to get you going.

■ ■ ■

Practice: Child's Pose

Asana is what most people think of when they first think of yoga, so let's try a simple asana here.

When you imagine asana, you might picture people standing in "warrior pose," or balancing on one foot in "tree pose," or standing on their head. But these represent just a small portion of the poses found in yoga. One of my absolute favorite yoga poses is child's pose. Also known as wisdom pose, it's a practice that can give us rest while also giving extension through the spine and a gentle stretch through the thighs, ankles, and tops of the feet.

When I'm teaching yoga, I offer child's pose early on. I tell my students that at any point during class, if they need a break, aren't feeling whatever we're working on, or just feel like it, they're welcome to do child's pose. It's yoga, not high school—do what you want!

Here's how to do child's pose.

1. Start on your hands and knees.

2. Untuck your toes so the tops of your feet sit on the yoga mat. (If you don't have a yoga mat, that's okay, but you should consider getting one, as they define your space for doing yoga and, more important, minimize the chance of your slipping.)

3. Bring your big toes together and your knees out a little wider.

4. Shift your hips back toward your heels. Allow your forehead to rest gently on the mat/floor.

5. If it's comfortable, allow your eyes to close.

That's it. That's a basic version of child's pose.

I like to offer variations of poses in my classes, so here are some possible ideas:

Try the pose without the big toes touching. Or bring the knees closer together so the belly can rest on the thighs. You can keep the hands extended out long or stack them underneath your forehead as a gentle pillow. If you are feeling tight through the shoulders, walk your hands back toward your ankles. Roll a blanket underneath the feet if you need added support there, or place a cushion under your seat if your hips feel uncomfortable.

Play around with lots of variations. See what works for you. Spend an entire yoga class in child's pose if you wanna, and if the teacher yells at you, find a different class!

Congratulations, you're doing yoga!

tl;dr

Get down on your hands and knees. Untuck your toes, bring your knees out a little wider, and shift your hips back to your heels. Rest your forehead on the earth and take a moment in child's pose.

22.

I Don't Wanna Grow Up

A FEW YEARS BACK, I was in Cleveland, sitting backstage with my band and some old friends who had come out to see us. Our friend Mikey asked how I was doing.

"I feel old," I said.

I was referring to how I couldn't quite party like I used to or stay up super-late or deal with the thousand cigarettes that were being smoked in the room. I'll never forget Mikey's response.

"I'm actually really enjoying aging."

It had never occurred to me that aging could be enjoyable, but Mikey was on to something. Getting older doesn't have to be a scary thing; if we see it for what it really is, it can be pretty sweet. Enjoying aging helps you enjoy today as it actually is, rather than how you think it should be. After all, with each moment comes a choice: will we try to cling to the past or find acceptance—happiness, even—in the present?

Western society has an obsession with youth: the products we're sold, the movies we watch, the music we listen to—they all make it seem like youth is about the best thing in the world. So it's no surprise that so many of us undergo plastic surgery, use weird chemicals, try crazy diets, and spend so much in our futile attempt to hold on to youth.

Youth-obsessed thinking seeps into all corners of life, even punk rock.

I always loved punk rock because it dared to question the norm. Thanks to punk rock, I've been exposed to all kinds of different ways to look at politics, social values, music and art, even food. But punk rock really falls in line with mass culture when it comes to youth. For so many punks, being young is the only way to be. My favorite bands have songs all about not wanting to grow up, being a Teenage This or a Teenage That, and living fast/dying young. Is getting older so bad that we'd really rather die?

Frankly, this whole obsession with youth can get really—you guessed it—*old*. And this is coming from a guy in a band full of dudes all in their thirties and forties called Teenage Bottlerocket. (If you just thought how funny it would be to refer to us as "Middle-Age Bottlerocket," well, you'd hardly be the first, but we love you anyway.)

With age comes change, of course, and we all have our hesitancies and fears about change. But change isn't all bad! Yes, most of us get a little squishier with age, a little hairier in some places and less hairy in others. I myself find that despite all my years of yoga, I'm not quite as flexible anymore. And I know things are only going to continue that way for the rest of my life.

That's okay. I'd still rather be here than where I was in the past.

When I was young, I thought it'd be a good idea to pierce my ears with a fork, then stretch the holes with drumsticks. If you ever meet me in real life, you might notice I still have holes about the size of a pen in both lobes. "Like cat buttholes" is one way they've been described to me. That was far from the only thing I was stupid enough to have pierced outside of a professional setting. (I'll leave the rest to your imagination.)

And that's just one example of (the *many*) dumb-shit things I did when I was younger. So what's my point?

Think of all the dumb shit *you* did as a kid. Really, take a moment now and think back. I'll bet there's some *super*-dumb shit in the memory bank. A lot of it might seem funny now, or gross, or kind of sad. The point is, we all did dumb shit, and might even still do some dumb shit, but one thing is for sure: we might be less flexible or squishier or whatever these days, but we are *wiser*. With age comes experience and wisdom.

Don't let that feed your ego, though. There's always something to learn, always room for growth. It just so happens that today you're at your wisest yet!

The ancient yogis understood that there was value in aging. Life was seen in stages, or *ashrama*. In the first stage—from birth to around age twenty-four—you grow up and you learn. You're a student of life itself. After that, you transition into the second phase of life and do things like raise a family and create a stabler existence for yourself.

At around age forty-eight, they believe, you retire. (Yeah, I know that seems early—and AWESOME.) Now, with all your time freed up, you get to spend some of it imparting your wisdom to the younger generation. Finally, at around age seventy-two you would, according to the ashrama concept, renounce everything you have, bail into the woods, and spend the remainder of your days on a spiritual quest for knowledge.

These age groupings don't really seem relevant to society today, and honestly, I look at them as just numbers. The important thing about the ashrama idea is that it recognized each stage of life as a part of an evolution and saw each stage as always valuable. Because of this, the ancient yogis knew to let go of the past and appreciate aging.

One big hindrance to our enjoyment of aging is our perspective: we have an idea of what getting old "should" look like, as opposed to how it actually is. If you think getting older means you have to stop dyeing your hair blue, wearing band T-shirts, or blasting Lagwagon records, you're wrong. If you think that because you're getting old, you need to make sure you do all those things so that you'll "stay" young, that's wrong too. What's right is to do what you want, within reason, and without doing harm.

What aging is really about is the accumulation of wealth—by which I don't mean money but the truly valuable things like wisdom and openheartedness. Today more than ever, you have tools available to you to help you learn, grow, love, and appreciate. You have the inspiration of those who inspire you. You have what you've been taught. You have this awesome book. You can thank aging for all this abundance. Sure, you might have to more actively take care of yourself, but that is a matter of perspective: do we *have* to ride our bikes, or do we *get* to ride our bikes?

Getting old usually comes with challenges: our bodies begin to experience more pain, we lose more and more people we love, we are unable to do all we used to do, and we may spend extended time in hospitals or nursing homes. I'm not trying to say some of these things aren't a *huge* bummer. What I am trying to say is that the bummerness is normal. It happens to all of us, pretty much (if we don't die first). Our perspective on these challenges can transform our lives, and maybe, just maybe, we can find some appreciation. These days, I live a slightly calmer life than I used to. I enjoy taking care of myself, my house, my business, and not partying my ass off every day. I still cut loose from time to time—and I certainly don't regret how things were in my past—but I'm older and I'm happier. It takes energy to cling to the past and fight getting older, and all that energy is wasted. It's much easier to just appreciate. So let's appreciate that today we're not as dumb as we used to be and we have more wisdom and love than ever before. Here's a practice to help make that appreciation stick.

■ ■ ■

Practice: That One Remembrance

Pierce your ears with a fork, then stretch the holes out with a drumstick.

Just kidding.

Do you recall the five remembrances, from a few chapters back? They break down the nature of impermanence into five steps. Let's revisit those quickly:

I am of the nature to grow old.

I am of the nature to get sick.

I am of the nature to die.

All that is dear to me and everyone I love are of the nature of change; I will be separated from them.

My actions are my only belongings; I cannot escape their consequences.

This time, we're going to focus on just the first one, *I am of the nature to grow old,* and reflect on why that is actually a great thing.

As always, first find your quiet sitting space. Take your seat, and breathe in and out. Spend several minutes in this simple, quiet meditation to clear your head and open your heart to the first remembrance.

1. *I am of the nature to grow old.* Say this to yourself quietly and sit with whatever comes up. Does it feel heavy? Sad? Light? Joyful? Whatever your initial reaction is, that's totally fine. Sit with it. See if you can't find acceptance. We all grow old. It's an undeniable truth.

2. Say it to yourself again: *I am of the nature to grow old.* Okay, so is that really such a bad thing? After all, today you have more experience and knowledge than you have ever had. Begin to expand acceptance into appreciation. Think of all of the benefits that come with aging.

3. Repeat again: *I am of the nature to grow old.* This "you" today is the best version of you that has ever existed. You are the culmination of everything that has happened to get you here, today. You are exactly where you are supposed to be.

4. One more time: *I am of the nature to grow old.* If we can embrace this truth, we can celebrate life as it is. Reflect on this for a few more moments, and then begin to release any thoughts.

5. Return to your normal breath, and after a few moments, open your eyes.

tl;dr

I am of the nature to grow old. Say this to yourself and observe what comes up. As best you can, find some softness in this truth. *I am of the nature to grow old.*

Now get your old ass up and go enjoy your day!

23.

Bare-Bottom Thanking

I WOKE UP JUST NOW in a band-wagon bunk on my way to Dallas to start TBR's latest tour.

I didn't really sleep well because the drive was long and bumpy.

I kind of have to take a dump, but I can't because there's no pooping on this bus.

I miss my dogs.

I miss my wife.

I miss my bed.

Still, my feeling this morning is one of gratitude: I'm grateful to have a bunk, grateful to be out here with my friends, grateful we still get to go on tour. Tonight, I get to have dinner with my dad. There have certainly been much worse days than today.

So I'm grateful. There's always something to be grateful for, even on the worst days.

I know there is a lot to complain about; no one would blame you if you did. Just look around. There are a million fucked-up things going on all the time, all over the world: war, mass shootings, social injustices, environmental disasters, the very dividedness of our society. . . . And our day-to-day lives aren't exactly bullshit-free either: bills, health problems, troubled family members, death. Life is hard. There's no denying that.

But if we're honest, there's no denying that life is also beautiful—even when things seem their worst. We just have to take a moment and look.

Of course, it's much easier (in a lazy way) to complain instead. But there's freedom in gratitude. Gratitude is perhaps the most effective, most transformative way of connecting. Through gratitude, a seemingly ordinary day, or even a bad one, becomes a perfect one.

Why wouldn't you want to go for that?

IF WE WANT TO HAVE A PERFECT DAY, we first need to solve the real problem. And here's the thing: it's not that there isn't anything to be grateful for; it's that we choose to focus on other things instead. We might, for example, take the easy way out and play the victim: We work hard but don't get what we want in return. We try to be nice, but people are assholes to us anyway. We just want to be happy, but bad things keep happening to us.

The world doesn't owe us anything; it never did and never will. We're wasting our energy on a fantasy. In fact, this unearned victim mentality is the true enemy. It's part of the ego's game: *poor me.* It keeps us stuck, feeling sad for ourselves, and that keeps us in disconnect. Now, I'm not saying that you can't feel bad or sad. There are plenty of legitimate reasons to feel those ways. But don't fall prisoner. Feel what you need to feel and then move forward. You can do that by returning to gratitude.

LET'S TURN AGAIN to those ancient, old-ass yogis for some insight. As discussed previously, the *niyamas* have to do with how we look at and work with our inner landscape. In these moments of observance we can, if we choose to, find *santosha*, or contentment. That means accepting things exactly as they are, here and now.

Remember that this moment can only truly exist as it is, not as what we think it is or think it should be. Our acceptance of that fact can have a huge impact on our sense of connection. If you can accept life as it is, rather than struggling and wishing for something else, you can settle down and find appreciation. That appreciation is just one step away from acceptance. There is literally always something, no matter how small it may seem, to be grateful for.

For starters, you are *breathing*. Each breath in means that you are still *receiving* in this life, and each breath out means that you are still *giving*. Even if my mom, my sister, my best friend, and my bandmate are each deceased, I am *still here*. It may hurt like hell sometimes, but I have lived to see another day.

And this day can be perfect, if my eyes and heart are open to it. This day can be Thanksgiving, if I'm open to it. A brief moment of silence can just be Thanksgiving, too, if I'm open to it. Often gratitude really just is a simple matter of acknowledgment and perspective. "Oh shit, it's raining, and this sucks" can turn into "I am thankful for this rainfall, which is nourishing the trees in my neighborhood and making it easier for me to breathe." Or, "Damn it, the neighbors' party is so loud" can turn into "I'm glad they're having fun and enjoying each other's company."

Another beautiful thing about gratitude is that we can come back to it again and again throughout our day. And each time we do, we are strengthening our connection to the present moment. It takes practice, of course. Luckily, I've got one for you.

■ ■ ■

Practice: A Moment of Thanks

This is a super-simple practice, one you can do again and again throughout the day. After enough repetitions it might even become second nature. Try it whenever you think of it, and see how your perspective begins to transform. All you'll need is a moment when something you don't like happens—which we all know can be pretty frequent. Here's what to do when it happens to you.

1. Pause. Rather than going down the rabbit hole of dissatisfaction, just pause.

2. Take a full breath in and a full breath out.

3. Find something about the situation to be grateful for. It might not be so obvious at first, but I promise, there is *something*. Even if the situation seems terrible, there's still a lesson that can be learned—or a much worse scenario that you *aren't* faced with. If nothing else, you are still alive. There is absolutely something.

4. Say to yourself silently, *I am thankful that* _____ . (You fill in the blank.) Then do your best to let go of any negativity while you move forward with your day.

That's it. It's that simple. See what happens when instead of indulging your anger or sadness or disappointment, you pause for gratitude instead.

tl;dr

Next time something seemingly undesirable happens, pause before giving yourself over to any particular type of reaction. Take a full breath. Ask yourself, is there something—anything—about the situation, this actual moment, to be grateful for? (Hint: there probably is.)

24.

Even on the Worst Nights

"What's the worst that could happen?"

There's a whole cottage industry that's built up around answering that question with "Worst-Case Scenario" books. Like zombie movies, they're kind of fun. But, these days, the *real* potential worst seems pretty fucking bad for more and more of us:

You could be barred from entering the country because of your religious beliefs or where you come from. You could have to risk everything to try to make a better life for your family, only to be detained, humiliated, and sent straight back. You could be fighting with every ounce of your being to try to protect our environment and our planet, only to have some climate change–denying billionaires fuck everything up beyond repair anyway.

The worst-case scenario can be pretty fucking terrible. We all know this to be true; it's right there in the name!

But there is another truth. It might not be easy to connect to and believe, but it's still true: *no matter how completely fucked things seem, you can still be okay.* As long as you have another moment on this planet and breath in your lungs, you can still find a way to move forward.

Even as I write this, I keep fixating on various scenarios:

What if my business fails, I am unable to pay my loans, and I lose my home? Hopefully won't happen, but could. *What if the fear and hate that is dividing this country leads to a mass revoking of green cards and my wife is deported?* I don't want to think about that! But it *could* happen. *What if some hateful, power-hungry zillionaires start a nuclear war, destroying the earth, and ending the human race?* Surely, *that's* the worst-case scenario.

Only, it isn't. The *actual* worst-case scenario would be to get so stuck worrying about what the worst-case scenario could be that my whole actual life passes me by.

If we're going on the basis that now is the only real moment, that past and future are an illusion, then the worst-case scenario can only happen *now*. And *now*, in *this* moment, my business is surviving. In *this* moment, my wife is here. Although the *threat* of nuclear war is real, as of right now as I write this book, it hasn't actually happened.

W HEN I THINK OF the worst-case scenario, death is often a key player. After all, it's ultimately inevitable. Losing my mom, my sister, Brandon, and other friends and family was horrific, but then the real worst case would have been never to have had them in my life at all.

To actually start healing, I would have to finally let myself feel what I had been trying not to feel for so many years: complete, absolute heartbreak. You see, aversion was keeping me from being happy. I was working so hard to avoid feeling pain that I was unable to fully enjoy the things I had to celebrate. It didn't matter that the band was doing great, and I was living out my childhood dreams; I was unable at the time to fully enjoy it. At some point

I hit bottom. I realized that even though everything in my external life seemed to be going so well, I was miserable and something needed to change. I knew then that I was going to have to face my pain to move forward. When I finally did let myself feel it all, I saw: it was okay. I was okay. Facing my feelings rather than running away helped me work through my suffering and emerge with a fuller heart than before.

We all have something to lose: friends, family, some sense of stability, a place to live; you might have to face the illness or death of people around you, or even your own. But even when we're face to face with our worst-case scenario, we can move forward. Heartbreak and loss don't have to destroy us. We can use them to connect.

The reason you can feel heartbreak is because you have a heart. Your heart is also a source of even strength and resilience, allowing you to handle more than you think you can, even your worst-case scenario, with loving-kindness. Here—you can prove it to yourself right now.

■ ■ ■

Practice: Tonglen Expanded

Let's revisit and expand on the tonglen practice from a few chapters back. As you might remember, the practice here is to sit with discomfort and let go of things we would normally cling to. Let's start by refreshing our memories.

Find your quiet spot to sit, and breathe for a little as you begin to clear your mind and open your heart to the practice of tonglen.

You'll recall that in the earlier, "bare-bones" version of tonglen, we worked with breathing in hot, heavy, uncomfortable air. We may have used this as a chance to visualize pollution or the sadness or suffering of someone else. On our out-breaths we imagined the air as cool and refreshing, visualizing bringing relief to someone other than ourselves. Work through these same two breaths for several moments. Now we will expand on this foundation we've set up.

1. Start to recall a painful situation. Again, we should work in steps so as to not overwhelm ourselves. Maybe on our first go it will be easier to recall the disappointment of losing a job than the sadness of the death of a loved one. Just find something you can manage working with—but also remember that you are stronger than you might think.

    As you hold this situation in your mind's eye, you may wish to set an intention that your tonglen practice may benefit not only you but also others who are faced with similar situations. Remember, you are not alone, no matter how much it might seem like it. Someone else has felt what you feel. Maybe the details of your stories are unique, but the pain of loss is universally felt. Holding this intention that our practice may benefit others as well as ourselves, we begin.

2. Breathing in, imagine absorbing all of the pain and suffering associated with this situation. Let yourself face the discomfort of doing so head-on, rather than indulging the usual reaction of hiding or "changing the subject" by engaging in daydreaming.

3. Then, as you breathe out, imagine the air as a healing, nurturing force—a gift. Send this gift out into the

world, and imagine the pain of your situation drifting away with it.

4. Repeat. Stay with this breath for several moments, taking in all of the pain and discomfort and then putting out healing, nurturing air. (I like to imagine my heart as a filter: no matter how much pain or bullshit is coming in, my heart can purify it and turn it into something positive.) When you've practiced this breath for several moments, begin to let go of it.

5. Return to the breath: in, out, simple.

tl;dr

Sit quietly and recall a painful situation. Start with a simple, manageable one, not one of the worst that's ever happened to you. Breathing in, "absorb" all of the pain associated with this situation. Face the pain directly. Let your heart filter the pain, by envisioning it turning into a healing, nurturing force, and exhale that out into the world.

25.

Rest in Peace

EVEN A PERFECT DAY can't last forever. But let's not let this one go just yet.

The end of the day is a good time to reflect upon the benefits of our practice. *How did today go? Did I recognize opportunities? Did I take them? Did I pour myself into whatever I was doing? Was I kind? Did I let things go when that was what was called for?*

As you look back on your day, there might be things you wish you would've done differently. Maybe you lost your temper or forgot something on your to-do list. Don't dwell on these things too much. Make note of how that could have gone differently, then fuck it and move forward.

There may also be things you feel happy about. Maybe you did great work today or had a special connection with a loved one. Maybe you took a moment of silence for yourself. Look for it and you'll see: there's something to be grateful for.

Then, let go of that too.

A perfect day ends by letting go of it all and making room for the next one: tomorrow.

You might want to just go to bed, but there's one last practice to do first. Don't worry—it's so easy you could practically do it in your sleep.

■ ■ ■

Practice: Corpse Pose

At the end of every yoga class we practice a "corpse pose." It's a restorative pose meant to help us unwind and absorb the benefits of our practice. Since our whole day can be a practice, I have included corpse pose here as the cherry on the sundae. Corpse pose can be a very relaxing place, or for those who find it hard to sit still, it can be challenging. Often those who resist corpse pose are the ones who could benefit the most. Give it a shot, see where you land, and know that, as always, either way is okay.

1. Find a quiet room, free from distractions. Floor space is important here, so make sure you have plenty of it.

2. Now, lay down flat on your back. Allow your legs to extend out long and your arms to rest down by your sides.

3. Close your eyes and get comfortable. Soften the muscles in your face, let your tongue relax away from the roof of your mouth. Let the back of your head be fully supported by the surface beneath you; your shoulders held up by the earth. Take a moment for any final wiggles or movements you need to make yourself 10 to 15 percent more comfortable and relaxed.

4. Now breathe. Breathe a simple nourishing breath in, allowing yourself to receive the gifts today has brought. Breathe out, allowing yourself to release anything that didn't serve you or go well today. Slowly,

let go of control over the breath, and let any sticky thoughts go too.

5. Allow yourself to rest in silence. That's it. There is nothing left to do. Today has been a good day, and tomorrow can be too. Stay here for as long as you'd like, maybe even a little longer than you normally would.

If you'd like to experiment with corpse pose, there are some modifications you can try. The goal is to let go completely, and the use of some props can help. An eye pillow might help you draw inward. If you're feeling tight through the lower spine, you might take a bolster or pillow under your knees. A blanket rolled gently under your neck can be a nice support for the head, or you can even completely cover yourself with a blanket if that helps you relax.

tl;dr

Lie down on your back with legs extended long, arms resting by your sides. Let the back of your head and the back of the shoulders relax into the floor. Let your hands and feet fall however they may want to fall. Let your eyes close as you return to a gentle, simple breath. There is nothing left to do but to rest here in corpse pose, breathing and absorbing the benefits of your practice.

26.

Your Perfect Day (Reprise)

ALRIGHT, here we are. The end of the book. Thanks for hanging in with me.

Now, let's wrap this shit up and get on with our lives.

Speaking of our lives, that reminds me of a question we asked at the beginning of this book, and just kept asking, really: *What in the fuck are we doing here anyway?*

Perhaps no one can say. But I think we can all agree, it's better when we really *live* our lives, and not just float through them.

We've seen, now, how the past and the future don't really exist (at least not how we've always thought they do). If that's true and we want to truly live our lives, it has to be now. Each new today is *our* day—and the kinds of reconnecting practices we've talked about here can help us make it a perfect one.

What would your perfect day look like? Perhaps no one can say that, either. Yes, there's a huge difference between how we think things should be and how they actually are. But as we've seen, we can find and connect to the beauty of life as it really is, even when everything sucks. There is always something to connect to, something to be grateful for. Doing that all day long? That's a perfect day.

As you head toward and into your perfect day, remember that it's *about* connection—to the moment, to the world around you—and everything starts with connecting to yourself. The practices in this book have helped me do that, and I hope they are helpful to you.

There are many other helpful practices out there too. Whatever really helps you connect to life, stick with it. Use your practices. Use them when things are comfortable. Use them when everything sucks. Even at the darkest moments, there is something worth living for. It's not something that's only found in the past or the future. It's you, now. So let yourself feel the dark times. But also be open to the relief that comes with the work of cultivating calmness and openheartedness.

Whatever the day may bring, you're ready for it—suckage, perfection, and everything in between.

Be well, my friend.

Some Recommended Reading

Dharma Punx: A Memoir, by Noah Levine

Everyday Zen: Love & Work, by Charlotte Joko Beck

The Four Agreements: A Practical Guide to Personal Freedom, by Don Miguel Ruiz and Janet Mills

Light on Yoga: The Classic Guide to Yoga, by BKS Iyengar

Lovingkindness: The Revolutionary Art of Happiness, by Sharon Salzberg

Tonglen: The Path of Transformation, by Pema Chödrön

The 12-Step Buddhist: Enhance Recovery from Any Addiction, by Darren Littlejohn

The Yamas & Niyamas: Exploring Yoga's Ethical Practice, by Deborah Adele

Acknowledgments

MIGUEL would like to thank his beautiful wife, Lily; his co-writer, Rod; his father, Benito; his brothers in Teenage Bottlerocket; Josh Bartok, Lydia Anderson, and everyone at Wisdom Publications; Tattooed Boy for the illustrations; all of his friends and family all over this beautiful world; and you. Without you, it'd just be us.

ROD thanks Miguel, Josh Bartok, Maura, and you for making this book a reality. Also: RAMONES.

About the Authors

MIGUEL CHEN is the bass player for long-running punk-rock band Teenage Bottle-rocket. He is a meditation practitioner, a yoga instructor, and the owner of Blossom Yoga Studio in Laramie and Cheyenne, Wyoming. In addition to appearing in countless Teenage Bottlerocket press pieces, Miguel has been featured by *Lion's Roar* magazine, PunkNews, Full Contact Enlightenment, LionsRoar.com, *Modern Vinyl*, Chris Grosso's MindPod podcast, and more.

ROD MEADE SPERRY is the editor of *A Beginner's Guide to Meditation* and editorial director of LionsRoar.com and Lion's Roar Special Projects. He is a board member of Zen Nova Scotia, the Buddhist community he practices with in his home of Halifax.

What to Read Next
from Wisdom Publications

HARDCORE ZEN
Punk Rock, Monster Movies, and the Truth about Reality
Brad Warner

"*Hardcore Zen* is to Buddhism what the Ramones were to rock and roll: A clear-cut, no-bulls**t offering of truth."
—Miguel Chen, Teenage Bottlerocket

UNSUBSCRIBE
Opt Out of Delusion, Tune In to Truth
Josh Korda
Foreword by Noah Levine

"Josh Korda makes Buddhism relatable and fresh, weaves in neuroscience and psychology, and serves it all up with a heaping dollop of candor, fearlessness, and wit. This book is a how-to guide for people wanting to learn how to face demons, forge deeper connections, sit comfortably in their skin, and step away from the distractions of social media and mindlessness of consumerism—things we all know will never leave us satisfied. Tune in and unsubscribe."
—Cara Buckley of *The New York Times*

Wʜᴀᴛ's Wʀᴏɴɢ ᴡɪᴛʜ Mɪɴᴅғᴜʟɴᴇss (ᴀɴᴅ Wʜᴀᴛ Isɴ'ᴛ)
Zen Perspectives
Robert Rosenbaum and Barry Magid

"This book is the best thing I've read on mindfulness and the mindfulness movement."—David Loy, author of *A New Buddhist Path*

About Wisdom Publications

Wisdom Publications is the leading publisher of classic and contemporary Buddhist books and practical works on mindfulness. To learn more about us or to explore our other books, please visit our website at wisdompubs.org or contact us at the address below.

Wisdom Publications
199 Elm Street
Somerville, MA 02144 USA

We are a 501(c)(3) organization, and donations in support of our mission are tax deductible.

Wisdom Publications is affiliated with the Foundation for the Preservation of the Mahayana Tradition (FPMT).